Master the Game
Defender

Master the Game
Defender

Paul Broadbent and Andrew Allen

HODDER
EDUCATION
PART OF HACHETTE LIVRE UK

All photographs have been provided by Action Images Ltd.

Orders: please contact Bookpoint Ltd, 130 Milton Park, Abingdon, Oxon OX14 4SB. Telephone: (44) 01235 827720. Fax: (44) 01235 400454. Lines are open from 9.00–5.00, Monday to Saturday, with a 24-hour message answering service. You can also order through our website www.hoddereducation.co.uk.

British Library Cataloguing in Publication Data
A catalogue record for this title is available from the British Library.

ISBN-13: 978 034092 8394

First Published   2008
Impression number   10 9 8 7 6 5 4 3 2 1
Year   2012 2011 2010 2009 2008

Hachette Livre UK's policy is to use papers that are natural, renewable and recyclable products and made from wood grown in sustainable forests. The logging and manufacturing processes are expected to conform to the environmental regulations of the country of origin.

Typeset by Servis Filmsetting Ltd, Manchester.
Printed in Great Britain for Hodder Education, part of Hachette Livre UK, 338 Euston Road, London NW1 3BH by Cox and Wyman Ltd, Reading, Berkshire.

Contents

Introduction

Football is without doubt the most popular sport in the world. In a recent survey carried out by FIFA (Fédération Internationale de Football Association), the world football governing body, it was estimated that there are 265 million male and female players worldwide. A pleasing sign in this survey is the continuing growth of the women's game. Over recent years, girls' football in particular has seen a massive growth in popularity and has now become the fastest growing sport for girls.

For many young people, football is played in order to 'live the dream' of becoming a professional player. This only becomes a reality for a small percentage, so in most cases the appeal of the game is largely social and for pure enjoyment, with the added health benefit of increased fitness. Whatever the reason, all young footballers aspire to play at their highest level and full potential. It is not uncommon for a keen young footballer to go through their early playing career without the regular support of a qualified football coach. These players, however, are still keen to improve their skills and develop their game.

This book has been written to support players to reach their full potential, allowing all young footballers to develop their game, either on their own

or with their friends. Following the practices and drills within the book, reading the top tips and testing themselves at the end of each chapter will give young players the opportunity to increase their knowledge and develop their game.

It is widely accepted that the more you practise, the better your game will become. This applies to football just as much as it does to any other sport. Knowing the correct techniques, understanding and applying tactical elements and analysing team play will allow young players to develop their game and improve their chances of success.

This book is one of a series of four books covering four key positions within the modern game: Goalkeeper, Defender, Midfielder and Striker. Each book contains tips, drills, practices and techniques applicable to the respective positions. There are also chapters within each book that will be of general interest to all footballers, relating to fitness, diet, equipment and dealing with injuries, as well as advice on finding the right club.

Football can certainly be 'a beautiful game' as Pelé once famously stated. With careful physical and mental preparation, increased understanding of the game and relevant practice of skills and techniques, you can play your part in this wonderful sport. We hope you enjoy the book and that it helps you achieve your potential as a footballer.

Paul Broadbent and Andrew Allen

Part 1

Introducing the game

Chapter 1

Playing the game

THIS CHAPTER WILL:
- Explain the principles of play.
- Describe team formations and systems.
- Give an understanding of what it takes to become a defender.

Principles of play

Playing football is all about attacking and defending, individually and as a team. The principles of playing football depend on whether your team is in possession of the ball, or whether the other team has possession. If your team is in possession of the ball you will be concerned with the **attacking principles of play**. All the players in your team will support the attack, as a unit, with specific responsibilities for each player depending on their individual position and where the ball is at the time.

If your team is not in possession of the football, you will be concerned with the **defending principles of play**. All the players in your team will have defensive responsibilities, as a unit, with specific

Attack as a team

Defend as a team

responsibilities for each player, once again, depending on their individual position and where the ball is.

Attacking principles

Attacking principles of play are about players creating space and then making the most of this space as an individual and as a team. For this to happen, your team needs to be in possession of the football. For it to happen effectively you will need to consider the following points:

- creating space by spreading out – side to side
- creating space by spreading out – end to end
- one-touch play
- changing direction of play
- dribbling.

Creating space by spreading out – side to side

It is important to try to create space both in between and behind defenders and this should happen as soon as possible after your team gains possession. If it is done quickly, it gives the opposition little time to man-mark and cover each other. Players should try to see everything that is happening on the pitch as they spread out, and should not turn their back on the ball. Having stretched out side to side, your team should look to progress forward as quickly as possible.

Creating space by spreading out – end to end

Teams should try to spread out their players 'end to end' as well as 'side to side'. This requires the player furthest away from the ball to make a run towards it, creating space behind them to be used by other players running off the ball into the space. Overlapping runs create space, and can take place on the wings and in central positions.

One-touch play

One-touch play is an extremely effective attacking tactic as it does not allow the opposition time to pressurize you and your team-mates. One-touch play requires players to have an excellent understanding of support and movement on and off the ball. Quick one-touch play, coupled with good movement, can make it very difficult for defenders to mark players and keep a tight formation. The 'wall-pass' is a common one-touch play in football. Passing the ball to a team-mate who plays it back to you, one touch, as you go forward and exploit the space in front of you, is an effective pass for attacking play.

The wall-pass is a common one-touch play in football.

Another example of a one-touch, pass and move play that can be very effective is called 'third man running'. This involves three players – a passer, a receiver and a runner. The ball is played up to the receiver, laid off at an angle to the passer and played one touch into the path of the runner.

Third man running can be an effective attacking tactic.

Changing direction of play

Players with the ability to see and then deliver a long diagonal pass from wing to wing can create and set up an opportunity to exploit space. Another effective way of changing the direction of play occurs when players make cross-over runs, pulling defenders out of position and creating space behind them. Another example is reverse passing, with players changing the direction of play by running with the ball in one direction and passing it in the opposite direction.

Dribbling

Dribbling is a very exciting attacking principle and is often used in the last third of the pitch. A player who can take on, and beat other players, or draw in defenders, creates space if the ball is delivered at the right time for team-mates to exploit it. If a player can take on and go past a defender it also creates a numerical advantage for his team.

Good dribbling can often help to create goals.

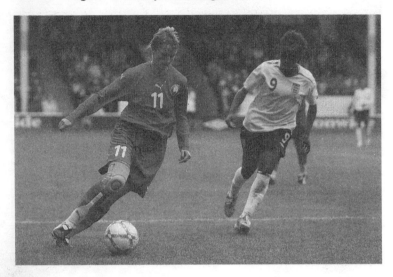

Defending principles

Defending principles of play are about denying the team in possession space. The defending team attempts to get all its players back behind the ball, applying pressure to the player in possession both individually and as a team. The following points are crucial to good defending:

* denying the opposition space
* applying pressure
* applying pressure, cover and balance.

Quote | 'If you've got pace, height, strength and can see danger then you're the all-round centre-back.'

Steve McClaren

Denying the opposition space

Two principles at the heart of good defensive play are **compactness** and **quantity**. In order to prevent the opposition from scoring, the defence has to be organized compactly, blocking the opposition's direct path to goal. Getting players back behind the ball and being compact as a unit makes it harder for the attackers to develop goal-scoring opportunities and generally forces them out to the wings. It is also important for the defending team to get as many players back behind the ball as possible, to outnumber the offensive players. This is why strikers and midfield players need to drop behind the ball when their team loses possession and for full-backs and other defenders to try to delay the attack by 'jockeying' so these players have time to run back.

Applying pressure

Pressurizing the ball is the first principle of defensive play, making it harder for the team in possession to develop their attacking play. Pressurizing the ball is most important when play is close to your own team's goal, to reduce the scoring opportunities. Successfully applying pressure, particularly as a team, often leads to regaining possession. The level of pressure is a decision that needs to be made by a defender in each situation. It may be that the defender needs to 'jockey' the player, delaying and slowing the player down until there are enough defenders to support and cover them. If the player is running with the ball in front of them it may be appropriate to carry out a well-timed tackle. Applying pressure in whatever form is a team responsibility. Without your team being able to shut or close down the outlet pass, there can be little point in individuals pressurizing the ball. An element of applying pressure involves 'marking' the attacking team players. This could mean staying very close to a specific player, or holding a formation so that if the ball comes into your area you get to the ball before an attacking player. Correct and thoughtful marking of players puts pressure on attacking players and denies them space to play.

Applying pressure, cover and balance

Pressure, cover and balance are the responsibilities of the first, second and third defenders. The **first defender** is the defender who is close enough to the ball to put pressure on the ball, possibly to tackle or to delay the attacker, denying them the opportunity to play the ball forward to their team-mates. This first defender may be a striker in your team. It will all depend on where the ball is at the time. The **second defender** is any defender who is close enough to cover space behind the first defender, who can step in and defend against the attacker if the first defender is beaten. All other players are **third defenders**. These are defenders who are not close enough to pressure the ball or to cover the space behind the first defender. Third defenders provide 'balance' so that, while other defenders apply pressure to try to win the ball, third defenders cover space on areas of the pitch away from the ball. Third defenders also track runners who run at space behind the defence.

Transition phase

Moving from defence into attack or attack into defence when possession changes is called the 'transition phase'. This can be a crucial part of the game. If a team is slow to get back to defend and set its defensive positions after it has lost the ball, the opposing team can quickly attack on the break, taking advantage of the space left on the pitch. Alternatively, a team that wins the ball and turns defence into attack needs its players to be quick-thinking, making decisive runs into attacking spaces. It is important that all players, in all positions, know their responsibilities as attackers and defenders. Concentration is important, so when there is a change of possession each player knows what his/her role is within the team, so that they act quickly and effectively.

Your role in a team

Whether your team is attacking (in possession) or defending (not in possession) you are likely to have certain responsibilities that will help

Full-back

Attacking	**Defending**
Give the team width in the back and midfield areas when your team is in possession.	Defend against opposing wide forwards and midfielders when the ball is on your side.
Look for opportunities to get forward to combine with outside midfielders down the wings.	Try to force the direction of play away from the goal, towards the wings.
When the ball is switched from one side to the other, try to exploit the space which will be available to you.	Try to prevent crosses from the wide areas.
	When the ball is on the opposite side of the pitch, balance the defence by tucking in towards the middle of the pitch.

your team. These responsibilities will vary, depending on the position you play in your team and also depending on where the ball is lost and regained.

Listed on page 11 and below are some of the responsibilities that you will have as a defender, depending on whether you are attacking or defending.

Central defenders or sweepers

Attacking	**Defending**
Help your team to keep possession by offering proper angle and distance of support to midfield players and full-backs.	Organize your team-mates all around you with effective communication.
Make good decisions with your pass selection – decide whether to play directly to forwards, or to play through midfield or to full-backs.	Assess whether you have marking responsibilities.
Be prepared to counter attack quickly by running the ball out of defence after winning possession.	Assess whether you are a supporting defender.

Team formations and systems

Team formations and systems are, in simple terms, how a team lines up at kick off and how they attempt to keep this team shape throughout the game. Coaches often ask what 'the best formation' is. There isn't one. A formation is supposed to make best use of the players' abilities within a team. What works best for a team depends on what their strengths are and what kind of players are available. It may also depend on factors such as playing against a strong attacking team or even weather conditions.

Top tips

- A good formation will help a good team, but skill and awareness count for much more.
- Whatever formation your team plays, it is vital that you stay in touch with all team-mates with good communication.
- Be prepared for your formation to change during a game – this decision will be made by your coach rather than the players.

This key applies to all formations shown in figures 1.3 to 1.7.

Key

GK	Goalkeeper	LM	Left midfielder
RB	Right-back	CM	Central midfielder
LB	Left-back	CF	Centre-forward
CD	Central defender	LF	Left-forward
RM	Right midfielder	RF	Right-forward

The 4–4–2 formation

The 4–4–2 formation is probably the most common one in the modern game, with a good balance throughout the positions. Four defenders and four midfielders will often mean eight players behind the ball when defending. The four midfielders are also available to support the two forwards when attacking. It can be an effective attacking formation, especially if you have two strong forwards who can outrun the opposition defence, and fast attacking midfielders to support them. However, with only two attackers playing up front, this alone is not enough to stretch apart a defensive line of usually four opponents. The two wide midfielders provide automatic width to the midfield and attacking shape of the team. The use of four defenders adds compactness and balance in the back, where either the sweeper or the flat back four can be utilized.

Figure 1.1 **The 4–4–2 formation**

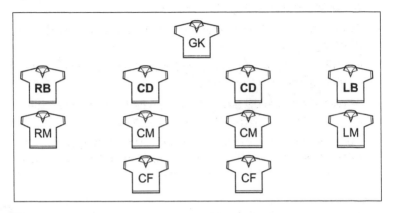

The role of the four defenders as a unit

The back four defenders must play as one unit wherever they are on the field of play, but particularly when they are in their defending half. Sometimes, teams will opt for the use of one central defender as a man-marker and the second central defender as a sweeper or covering defender, although it is not uncommon for teams to play with a 'flat back four' which sees both the central defenders sharing the responsibility for marking and covering.

Often teams will play this system as it is suitable for deploying offside trap tactics, though this requires teams to be exceptionally well organized and drilled, with communication being vital. The 4–4–2 formation also allows more freedom for the two wide defenders to attack.

As one of the **two wide defenders** (right back and left back) you should:

- Be part of one defensive unit, particularly in the defending half of the pitch.
- Have the ability to defend in 1 v 1 situations – understanding when to jockey and delay and when to challenge an oncoming opponent.

- Communicate with other defenders so the unit remains compact and does not get too spread out.

- Remain disciplined with defensive duties even when the team is attacking.

- Provide instant width, particularly for goalkeepers when building possession from the back.

- Be part of a unit in the wide channels, with the wide midfielder and wide forward when attacking or defending.

- Offer support to wide and central midfield players by providing an option of an overlap or a supporting position behind the ball in order for the team to keep possession.

As one of the **two central defenders** you should:

- Be part of the defensive unit, particularly in the defending half of the pitch.

- Have the ability to defend in 1 v 1 situations – understanding when to jockey and delay and when to challenge an oncoming opponent.

- Communicate with other defenders so the unit remains compact and does not get too spread out. The covering defender acts as a leader for communication to other defenders.

- Communicate with each other so you know when to mark and when to cover.

- Remain disciplined with defensive duties even when the team is attacking.

- Provide central cover when possession is being built from the back.

- Be part of a unit in the central areas with central midfielders and centre-forwards when attacking or defending.

- Offer support to all the midfield players by providing a passing option behind the ball in order for the team to keep possession.

The 3–5–2 formation

The 3–5–2 formation is more attacking than the 4–4–2 formation, as it moves forward the 'fourth full-back', who often may have minimal defending to do against only two attackers. With only three at the back, defenders must be solid and work together as a unit. Often a midfield player may be called upon to support the defence. A coach may consider a 3–5–2 formation if they have an abundance of midfield players. Like all systems it needs to be able to operate when defending and attacking. Using this formation, teams will often defend and attack in two units – the back three and the midfield five when defending, and the midfield five and two forwards when attacking.

Role of the three defenders as a unit

Generally, the three defenders will be out-and-out defensive players, mainly because there will be little opportunity for them to get forward, other than for set pieces, due to the minimum number of defenders. Most teams will organize themselves with two of the defenders man-marking the forwards and one defender acting as a sweeper or covering player. Some teams find alternative ways to defend using this system and

Figure 1.2 **The 3–5–2 formation.**

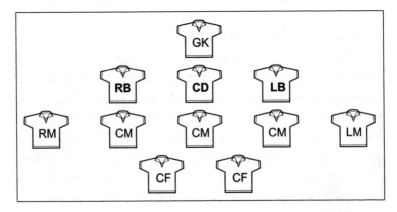

may opt for each defender being responsible for an area, marking or covering within that area. With only three defenders, some teams may use one of their central midfield players to play just in front of the back three defenders to try to cut out some of the dangerous play before it reaches the defence.

As one of the **three defenders** you should:

- Be part of one defensive unit, particularly in the defending half of the pitch.
- Communicate with other defenders so the unit remains compact and does not get too spread out. The covering defender acts as a leader for communication to the other defenders.
- Identify two defenders to mark players, while the third defender acts as a sweeper or covering player.
- Remain disciplined with defensive duties even when the team is in attack.
- Make sure the sweeper covers the full-backs and picks up any loose balls.
- Make sure that the sweeper has a good reading of the game and is confident in distributing the ball from these defensive positions. Occasionally, the sweeper will have the opportunity to bring the ball out of defence and set up a fast break.

The 4–5–1 formation

The 4–5–1 and 4–3–3 formations are very similar, with the 4–5–1 being a defensive set-up that can easily switch into a 4–3–3 if necessary. The nature of the positioning of the players makes it a very difficult system to break down, particularly if the team remains well organized and disciplined. With the midfield packed and compact, it is good for keeping possession of the ball through a series of short passes, occasionally linking up with the lone forward. In attacking terms there is a real emphasis on the midfield players to get forward to support the lone

Figure 1.3 **The 4–5–1 formation**

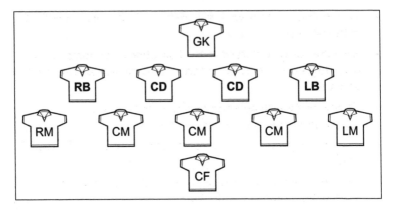

striker. The wing backs (wide midfield players) provide instant width in attack and good defensive cover in these wide positions. The wing backs can also be used to bring the ball out of defence. The system may see the back four defenders playing with a sweeper or a 'flat back four'.

The role of the four defenders as a unit

The back four defenders must play as one unit wherever they are on the field of play, but particularly when they are in their defending half. Sometimes, teams will opt for the use of one central defender as a man-marker and the second central defender as a sweeper or covering defender, although it is not uncommon for teams to play with a 'flat back four' which sees both the central defenders sharing the responsibility for marking and covering.

Often teams will play this system as it is suitable for deploying offside trap tactics, although this requires teams to be exceptionally well organized and drilled, with communication being vital. The 4–5–1 system also allows more freedom for the two wide defenders to support the attack.

As one of the **two wide defenders** (right back left back) you should:

- Be part of the defensive unit, particularly in the defending half of the pitch.

- Have the ability to defend in 1 v 1 situations – understanding when to jockey and delay and when to challenge an oncoming opponent.

- Communicate with other defenders so the unit remains compact and does not get too spread out.

- Remain disciplined with defensive duties even when the team is attacking.

- Provide instant width, particularly for goalkeepers when building possession from the back.

- Be part of a unit in the wide channels, with the wide midfielder and wide forward when attacking or defending.

- Offer support to wide and central midfield players by providing an option of an overlap or a supporting position behind the ball in order for the team to keep possession.

As one of the **two central defenders** you should:

- Be part of the defensive unit, particularly in the defending half of the pitch.

- Have the ability to defend in 1 v 1 situations – understanding when to jockey and delay and when to challenge an oncoming opponent.

- Communicate with other defenders so the unit remains compact and does not get too spread out. The covering defender acts as a leader for communication to other defenders.

- Communicate with each other so you know when to mark and when to cover.

- Remain disciplined with defensive duties even when the team is attacking.

- Provide central cover when possession is being built from the back.

- Be part of a unit in the central areas with central midfielders and centre-forwards when attacking or defending.
- Offer support to all the midfield players by providing a passing option behind the ball in order for the team to keep possession.

The 4–3–3 formation

Teams playing a 4–3–3 formation are likely to be playing a narrow game, through the middle of the pitch, although when the ball is on their side of the pitch, the full-back and wide midfield player should be encouraged to take up wide positions to provide width in the attack. The two full-backs are able to provide automatic width when building play from the back. With 4–3–3, teams need to encourage the wide forwards to drop back to help with the build-up. One of the benefits of this formation for younger players is that they often look to force the ball through the middle of the field, whereas this system encourages them to build attacks by playing the ball forward into the wide channels rather than simply through the middle.

Figure 1.4 **The 4–3–3 formation**

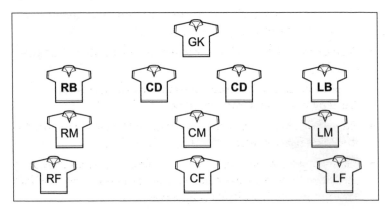

The role of the four defenders as a unit

The back four defenders must play as one unit wherever they are on the field of play, but particularly when they are in their defending half. Sometimes, teams will opt for the use of one central defender as a man-marker and the second central defender as a sweeper or covering defender, although it is not uncommon for teams to play with a 'flat back four' which sees both the central defenders sharing the responsibility for marking and covering.

Often teams will play this system as it is suitable for deploying offside trap tactics, although this requires teams to be exceptionally well organized and drilled, with communication being vital. The 4–3–3 formation also allows more freedom for the two wide defenders to attack.

As one of the **two wide defenders** (right back and left back) you should:

- Be part of one defensive unit, particularly in the defending half of the pitch.
- Have the ability to defend in 1 v 1 situations – understanding when to jockey and delay and when to challenge an oncoming opponent.
- Communicate with other defenders so the unit remains compact and does not get too spread out.
- Remain disciplined with defensive duties even when the team is attacking.
- Provide instant width, particularly for goalkeepers when building possession from the back.
- Be part of a unit in the wide channels, with the wide midfielder and wide forward when attacking or defending.
- Offer support to wide and central midfield players by providing an option of an overlap or a supporting position behind the ball in order for the team to keep possession.

As one of the **two central defenders** you should:

- Be part of the defensive unit, particularly in the defending half of the pitch.

- Have the ability to defend in 1 v 1 situations – understanding when to jockey and delay and when to challenge an oncoming opponent.

- Communicate with other defenders so the unit remains compact and does not get too spread out. The covering defender acts as a leader for communication to other defenders.

- Communicate with each other so you know when to mark and when to cover.

- Remain disciplined with defensive duties even when the team is attacking.

- Provide central cover when possession is being built from the back.

- Be part of a unit in the central areas with central midfielders and centre-forwards when attacking or defending.

- Offer support to all the midfield players by providing a passing option behind the ball in order for the team to keep possession.

The 3–4–3 formation

The 3–4–3 formation is considered to be an attacking formation when in possession of the ball, and also lends itself to a high-pressure style of defending without the ball. Using this formation, teams can easily attack and defend with a minimum number of seven players, either the back three and four midfield players when defending, or the midfield four and the three forwards when attacking. Normally the central striker will consistently stay at the tip of the attack while one midfield player will often protect the back three by constantly pressurizing the ball to help the defence.

Figure 1.5 **The 3–4–3 formation**

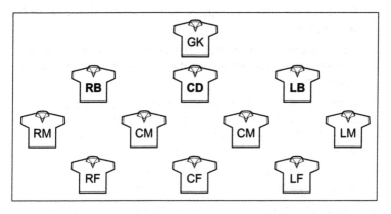

The role of the three defenders as a unit

Generally, the three defenders will be out-and-out defensive players, mainly because there will be little opportunity for them to get forward, other than for set pieces, due to the minimum number of defenders. Most teams will organize themselves with two of the defenders man-marking the forwards and one defender acting as a sweeper or covering player. Some teams find alternative ways to defend using this system and may opt for each defender being responsible for an area, marking or covering within that area. With only three defenders, some teams may use one of their central midfield players to play just in front of the back three defenders to try to cut out some of the dangerous play before it reaches the defence.

As one of the **three defenders** you should:

- Be part of one defensive unit particularly in the defending half of the pitch.
- Communicate with other defenders so the unit remains compact and does not get too spread out. The covering defender acts as a leader for communication to the other defenders.

- Identify two defenders to mark players while the third defender acts as a sweeper or covering player.

- Remain disciplined with defensive duties even when the team is in attack.

- Make sure the sweeper covers the full-backs and picks up any loose balls.

- Make sure that the sweeper has a good reading of the game and is confident in distributing the ball from these defensive positions. Occasionally, the sweeper will have the opportunity to bring the ball out of defence and set up a fast break.

What it takes to become a defender

Whatever your favoured position, or the position that you are asked to play in by your coach, you will need a range of technical, physical and psychological skills and attributes. Many of these are relevant to more than one position, for example, a good defender will also need to have the ability to get forward and join an attack, and so they will need to develop their skills and attributes to suit the demands of attacking play.

Quote | 'The qualities I see in a centre-half include the ability to head the ball in both boxes, pace, positional sense and confidence with the ball. But first and foremost I want them to be defenders – natural stoppers.'

David Moyes

From research and player observation, it has been identified that 'good defenders' are likely to have the attributes listed in the table on page 28, almost all of which can be developed and improved with practice and support from your coach.

The advantages and disadvantages of various formations

Table 1.1 **sets out the advantages and disadvantages of these five systems**

	3-5-2	4-4-2	4-3-3	4-5-1	3-4-3
Defensive strength	Usually one central midfielder sits in front of the back three. This gives good cover of central space.	Four players when defending, provides cover of all space.	Covers the space well. Also good for stopping opposition playing out from back.	Very strong defensive unit, but does depend on how many players are pushed forward to attack.	Good coverage of the central areas of defence, though without central support from midfield to sit in front of the back three.
Defensive weakness	Three defenders instead of four means 25 per cent extra space for two wide forwards to exploit.	Fewer players in the central areas.	Fewer players in the central areas and less support for full-backs on the transition phase.	Only one forward means the opposition have real opportunity to play the ball in their defensive third.	Even though strong centrally, extra space for two wide forwards to exploit.

Table 1.1 **(continued)**

	3–5–2	4–4–2	4–3–3	4–5–1	3–4–3
Playing out from the back	With only three at the back, wing backs need to drop back, though this then gives them fewer passing options.	The two full-backs start in excellent positions to offer this option to their team.	The two full-backs start in excellent positions to offer this option to their team, though less wide support for the next pass. Often sees teams playing a longer pass forward.	This formation provides several options, though the position will often push a full-back forward into midfield to try to counter this.	With only three at the back it does not offer the options for players to receive the ball in wide positions.
Effect on midfield	The central midfield area will often have a numerical advantage – three to two.	Provides a diamond or flat shape to the midfield when attacking or defending. If outnumbered in midfield, sometimes a full-back will be pushed into midfield.	The three midfield players are likely to be central, which means the team may require two of the forwards to drop back to help in the wider areas of the pitch.	This formation provides several options to the midfield – often three midfield players will support the forward (two wide and one central).	Provides a diamond or flat shape to the midfield. If outnumbered in midfield, it will require one of the forward players to drop back to support the midfield.

Effect on forwards	Provides good central support for runs beyond the forwards.	The midfield and full-backs need to be willing to get forward to support the forwards.	Numerically, it suggests that three forwards offer you more, although this depends on how much dropping back the two wide forwards have to do.	Really needs a forward who is good at holding the ball up and bringing the midfielders into the game.	Numerically it suggests that three forwards offer you more, although this depends on the amount of defensive duties required from the wide forwards.
Overall	Strong centrally and in central midfield. Vulnerable to width at the back.	Strong defensively and can be good for playing out from the back. Best formation for using the full width of the pitch.	Good for stopping opposition's full-backs from playing. Offers less width for playing out from the back, but can offer width in attack.	A relatively defensive formation. The team needs to be able to play well and have a forward who can hold the ball up well.	Strong centrally, in defensive areas, and good formation for using width in midfield. Three forwards provide width in attack.

Key attributes of a defender

	Centre-back	Sweeper	Full-back
Technique (when in possession)	Comfortable in possession. Natural right/left foot. Heading ability – 'flick-ons'.	Accurate passing. Ability to run the ball. Comfortable possession. Natural right/left foot.	Good passing technique. Crossing skills. Ability to receive the ball with both feet. Comfortable in possession. Natural right/left foot. Support players in possession.
Technique (when not in possession)	Heading ability – defensive. Strong tackler. Good defending 1 v 1.	Confident Support and cover for other players.	Confident tackler. Tracking back. Good defending 1 v 1. Stop crosses by 'jockeying'. Make play predictable.
Physical	Strength in the air. Reasonable speed. Quick reactions. Tough/strong.	Excellent speed. Quick reactions. Tough/strong.	Good speed. Turning ability. Fitness levels to join attack. Quick reactions. Tough/strong.
Mental/ psychological	Good tactical knowledge. Decisive. Disciplined. Anticipation. Brave. Ability to read the game.	Good communicator. Anticipation. Ability to read the game. Interception skills.	Positional sense. Patience. Competitive. Enjoys defending. Willingness to join the attack.

Summary

- Football is all about attacking and defending, and the transition between these. Whatever position you play you need to understand the attacking and defending principles of play.

- Players need to try to create space when attacking and deny space to the opposition when defending.

- You need to be clear about your roles and responsibilities in the team whether attacking or defending.

- A team formation, such as 4–4–2, shows the 'shape' that a team keeps throughout the game. Any formation needs to be flexible and make the best use of the players' abilities.

Self-tester

- Describe the tactic of 'third man running'.
- What is the role of the 'second defender'?
- What are the advantages of playing a 4–3–3 formation?
- Give three attributes of a good 'sweeper'.

Action plan

Using the attributes listed above, consider how you match up to the skills and attributes for the position you play. Use this book to find out how you can improve your technique and understanding for the position you play (Chapters 7, 8 and 9 will help you improve your game). With the support of your teacher or coach (and also Chapter 11 of this book), evaluate your performance and develop a goal-setting programme.

Part 2

Preparing for the game

Chapter 2

Fitness for football

THIS CHAPTER WILL:
- Give an understanding of the key elements that make up general fitness.
- Consider the specific elements of fitness that you need as a footballer.
- Outline the importance of exercise to keep fit.

You may know from experience that football can be a physically demanding sport. If you monitored the types of movements that you made during a match it would make an impressive list:

- sprinting
- jogging
- walking
- running backwards
- running sideways
- accelerating
- jumping
- kicking
- turning
- stretching.

All these will be very difficult if you don't have a basic level of general fitness as well as a specific fitness suited to football.

Statistic

A professional footballer runs between 8 and 13 kilometres in a match.

Quote | 'The majority of top defenders will be good athletes, quick, tall, strong in the air and good tacklers. If a defender does not have real pace, then they need to be able to read the game. John Terry, at Chelsea, is not the quickest defender in the premiership, but he makes up for any lack of pace with his reading of the game.'

Steve Clarke

The four Ss

Players with good skills, technique and motivation may be 'natural' footballers, but if they are short of general fitness they are unlikely to reach their potential. To be generally fit and healthy and able to do everyday physical activities without feeling tired, you need the four Ss:

- **Speed** – a big part of the game, not just for short sprints but also for longer concentrated spells.
- **Strength** – many skills in football can be helped with physical strength, in both the upper and lower body.
- **Stamina** – football is a high-intensity sport played over a long period and players need to last the full 90 minutes in a match.
- **Suppleness** – flexibility is important because of the wide range of movements required when playing football.

Figure 2.1 **The four Ss**

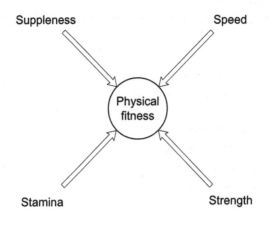

Suppleness

Speed

Physical
fitness

Stamina

Strength

Specific fitness

As well as a good level of general fitness, you need to have specific fitness to play football at a high level. The following are the elements of fitness that can make the difference between a good player and a world-class player:

- **Agility** – in a match you may turn and change direction 400–500 times, so you need to be able to move and turn quickly and easily.

- **Quick reactions** – you need to respond quickly to constant and sudden changes in play.

- **Balance** – with the ball at your feet, and an attacker putting you under pressure, you need to be balanced and steady in order to keep possession, pass or shoot.

- **Coordination** – there are a number of different techniques and movements involved in passing, shooting or tackling. These rely on different parts of the body working together smoothly and efficiently.

- **Timing** – you need to act at just the right moment, with good timing for your runs, tackles or passes.

There are also specific elements of fitness that players in different positions in a team will need. A goalkeeper will have different requirements from a midfielder, and even as a defender there are different roles depending on the type of defender you are – centre-back, sweeper or full-back.

Centre-back

Centre-backs need to be strong and quick as well as having the stamina to last for 90 minutes. They need physical strength to hold up and track target strikers. The position requires a lot of power (strength and speed) that is released in short bursts of energy, while under sustained spells of pressure. The centre-backs will also need good stamina and a quick recovery time so that they can make challenges, turns and sprints throughout the game.

Sweeper

The key attributes for this role are speed and strength. Sweepers need to be good 'readers' of the game, with quick reactions and excellent timing. They need to be quick to cover any through-balls that beat the defence in front of them, and they need to be strong to hold up and tackle strikers in front of goal.

Full-back

If you play as a full-back, it is likely that you are quick and possess good balance and agility. Speed is a key attribute for a full-back, for making attacking overlapping runs as well as tracking back for your defensive duties. This means you are likely to cover a lot of ground in a match, so excellent stamina is also necessary to keep going for the full 90 minutes.

Statistic

In the previous two World Cup finals more than 20 per cent of all the goals scored were in the last 15 minutes.

The importance of exercise

Fitness is obviously an important element if you want to play a good standard of football. When you were younger you may not have needed to exercise to keep fit; you naturally used up a lot of energy and kept fit in your daily routines and activities. As you get older, you will notice that you need to work a little harder to keep in good physical condition – and this is where regular exercise fits in. Exercise is good for you. It helps you to develop as a person, both physically and mentally.

On a **physical** level, exercise:

- improves your posture and body shape
- helps cardio-vascular fitness – keeping your muscles supplied with oxygen
- develops your muscle tone and strength
- strengthens your bones
- reduces your chance of illness.

On a **mental** level, exercise:

- helps relieve stress and tension
- increases self-confidence
- gives you a challenge
- gives you something to look forward to – it's fun!

Genetics plays a part; some people need very little exercise to maintain a high fitness level, while others need a daily physical activity to keep fit. Even though some seem to be born with a head start, this doesn't mean that other less naturally fit people cannot see massive improvements providing they train and work hard. If you stop any physical activity for a while, you will definitely notice the difference in your body and your state of mind. Get to know your body and your fitness levels.

- **At what times do you feel at your best?**
- **When do your energy levels feel low?**
- **How long does it take you to recover from exercise?**

The technical bit . . .

Whenever we exercise our respiratory system responds in obvious ways, such as shortness of breath and gasping for air. This is because the body uses more energy as we exercise, and our muscles demand more oxygen to maintain this energy level. The fitter we are through regular exercise, the greater our lung capacity and efficiency, and the less we gasp for breath.

Cardiovascular fitness involves keeping oxygen supplied to your muscles from your heart and lungs. Several things happen to your heart while you exercise. Your heart rate (beats per minute) goes up, increasing the speed at which your heart pumps blood, and oxygen, to your muscles. The stroke volume also increases, which is the amount of blood pumped from the heart during each beat. When you are exercising hard, your heart rate can go up to almost three times its resting rate. Well-trained athletes can have a resting rate as low as 30 beats, with most people having a resting heart rate of approximately 60 beats per minute. Reducing the recovery time of your heart rate after exercise to its resting rate is a good sign that you are improving your fitness.

Statistic
On average a heart beats approximately 86,400 times a day.

Sorting out a training programme

Your performance as a player can be improved by fitness training. There are five general training categories:

- **Aerobic** – endurance training, working your heart and lungs over a long time.
- **Anaerobic** – short, quick, powerful activities to build up muscles.
- **Strength** – weight training, developing specific muscles.
- **Flexibility** – active and passive stretching of muscles.
- **Skills** – improving skills and techniques, supporting specific fitness.

Your training programme is likely to be planned and organized by your coach. It needs to suit you, so make sure you talk to your coach, sharing your views. Answer these questions about yourself, as these will influence the type of programme you could have:

- How fit are you now?
- What exercises do you like?

- Do you have any injuries?
- What exercises do you dislike?
- Do you have any health problems?
- Are there any particular aspects you want to work on (speed, strength, stamina, suppleness)?

Your training will vary for each stage of the year:

- **Pre-season training** – aerobic, anaerobic, flexibility and skills training, with some strength training.
- **Training during the season** – maintain level of general fitness and rest after matches.
- **Recuperation** – rest and relax at the end of the season to recover from any injuries and fatigue, maintain flexibility.
- **Out-of-season training** – aerobic and strength training, maintain flexibility.

It is essential that a coach advises you on any training programme you undertake. They will consider the different fitness components, known as FITT:

Frequency – how often should the type of exercise be performed?
Intensity – how hard should the exercise be?
Time – how long should the exercise session be?
Type – what types of exercises should you use?

With the help of your coach you can develop a weekly fitness programme similar to the example below which is typical of a pre-season training programme. This is not in any particular order, and does not include warming up and cooling down:

Aerobic training	5 × 400 metres with 30 seconds recovery, or 5–10 km run.
Anaerobic training	10 × 20 metre shuttle followed by 30 seconds rest. 10 × 50 metre shuttle followed by 60 seconds rest.
Strength training	Squat jumps, press-ups, weights/resistance work in a gym.
Flexibility training	Careful stretching for each major muscle group.
Skills training	Working on specific skills.

Summary

- **The four Ss are fundamental components of fitness.**

- **Different playing positions require different physical attributes.**

- **Exercise has both physical and mental benefits.**

- **When you exercise, your heart rate (the number of beats per minute) and your stroke volume (amount of blood in each beat) both increase.**

Self-tester

- What are the four Ss of general fitness?
- What are the physical requirements of a full-back?
- Why do we get short of breath when we exercise?

Action plan

Think about a training plan for you for each part of the year. Talk about it with your coach and write it up as a weekly programme. Monitor your fitness each month to check progress.

Chapter 3

Food for a footballer

THIS CHAPTER WILL:
- Explain the importance of a healthy balanced diet.
- Give an understanding of what to eat and when.
- Examine the place of carbohydrates in a footballer's diet.

Quote | 'You are what you eat.'

This is a well-known phrase that shows the importance of food for our bodies. So what does it mean? It is basically saying that the food you eat has a direct effect on the type of person you are. If you want to lead a healthy lifestyle, stay fit and become physically strong so that you give your best in training and in matches, your diet really does matter.

Nutrients

All living things need food as the basic fuel for life. It keeps us warm, gives us energy and helps us grow. Our food and drink contains a variety of nutrients, including carbohydrates, fats and proteins. The aim is to try to get the right balance of these each day. Energy-giving foods contain carbohydrates and fats, which are burned up slowly by the body. Energy in food is measured in calories, and a high-calorie diet is needed if you exercise regularly and burn off the calories. Body-building foods that help us grow are high in protein.

Look at Table 3.1 below to find out a little more about different food types:

Table 3.1 **Food types**

Nutrient	What do they do?	Where do we get them from?
Carbohydrates	These are mainly stored in muscles as glycogen, used for energy. Great demands are placed on these carbohydrate stores during exercise.	Simple carbohydrates (sugars): sweets, cakes, soft drinks. Complex carbohydrates (starches): rice, bread, pasta, potatoes, cereal, fruit.
Fats	These are mainly stored in body tissues and muscles. They help produce energy.	Butter, margarine, oils, oily fish, cheese, whole milk, nuts.
Proteins	These are needed for the growth and repair of body tissues, and to help with the immune system.	Milk, cheese, meat, yoghurt, fish, eggs, nuts.
Vitamins and minerals	These play an important part in being healthy and feeling well.	Present in tiny quantities in natural foods: fruit, vegetables, nuts, fish, meat, eggs, dairy products, cereals.
Fibre	In the digestive system these help absorb and use nutrients.	Wholegrain cereals, fruit, vegetables, seeds, peas, beans.
Water	Performs many functions – essential for healthy living.	Foods, drinks.

A balanced diet

No single food contains all the nutrients we need, so it is important that we eat a wide variety. A balanced diet is one that gives the right mix to keep us healthy and fit.

Figure 3.1 shows examples of foods from the main food types, and the recommended proportion to be eaten each day.

Figure 3.1 **The daily recommended requirements of the major food groups**

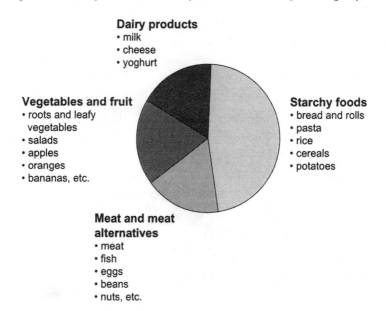

Dairy products
• milk
• cheese
• yoghurt

Vegetables and fruit
• roots and leafy
  vegetables
• salads
• apples
• oranges
• bananas, etc.

Starchy foods
• bread and rolls
• pasta
• rice
• cereals
• potatoes

**Meat and meat
alternatives**
• meat
• fish
• eggs
• beans
• nuts, etc.

Best food for football

Playing any level of football uses energy and will burn off calories. If you play at a competitive level, you can burn off between 600 and 800 calories during a match, so energy-giving food is needed in your diet. This means that it is best to increase the amount of carbohydrates you eat. Make sure they are mainly 'complex' carbohydrates, such as rice, bread, pasta, cereal and fruit, rather than the 'simple' sugary carbohydrates. The pie-charts in Figure 3.2 show the difference in diet between that recommended for a normal healthy person and that recommended for a sportsperson.

Figure 3.2 **The difference in recommended diet between a normal healthy person and a sportsperson**

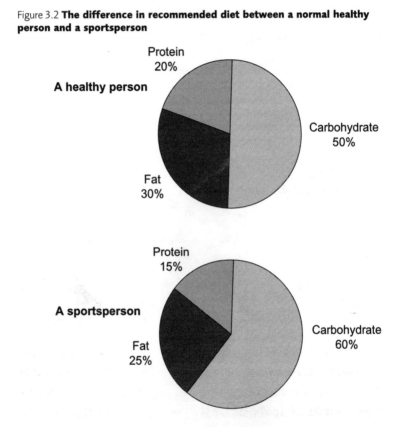

It is recommended that active footballers should get as much as 60–70 per cent of their daily diet in the form of carbohydrates. This is because the carbohydrate stores in your body can run out during exercise.

To ensure that your diet is high in carbohydrate and also 'balanced', a mixture of carbohydrate-rich foods and drinks should be consumed. If you have a good variety it will mean that you will take in enough of the other nutrients such as protein, vitamins, minerals and fibre. The following foods are rich in carbohydrates:

- breads, pizza bases
- rice, pasta and noodles
- potatoes and potato products
- peas, beans, lentils and corn
- fruit – fresh, dried and tinned
- sugar, jam and honey
- biscuits, cakes and buns
- muesli bars
- yoghurts and puddings
- sports drinks.

Top tip

Think about the types of food you **should** eat when you go shopping for food. Are there any changes you could make?

You need to eat three meals a day, but even then this may not be enough carbohydrate intake if you are active in sport. Therefore, snacking should play an important role in your nutrition programme. The following are popular snacks for footballers as they are high in carbohydrates and relatively low in fat:

- jam, honey, bananas, peanut butter sandwiches
- muesli bars, popcorn
- fruit cake, currant buns, scones

- crumpets, bagels, muffins
- cereal, rice pudding.

Think about the food you eat and the types of snacks you have. Could you alter any of them? Decide on the best times for you to eat snacks. Some footballers like to eat and drink straight after exercise, some like to have a drink and wait an hour or two before eating a snack or meal.

Top tip

Keep up your carbohydrate levels by eating sensibly at meal times and snacking sensibly throughout the day.

The importance of fluids

During training and when playing matches it is vital to drink regularly to maintain hydration. Feeling thirsty is a sign of being dehydrated, but by then it's a little late. By the time you are thirsty you are already partly dehydrated. If you finish a training session and you are thirsty then you have not taken enough fluid on board during the session. Whenever you become thirsty start to drink immediately. Preferably, drink before you are thirsty. Try not to drink too much in one go during a match or training. Drinking too much, too quickly, particularly if already dehydrated, can cause stomach upset.

Drinking plain water is not the most effective way to rehydrate, as drinks should contain moderate electrolyte levels (sodium and some potassium). Sports drinks are a good choice as they are specially made with the correct mix of carbohydrates, fluid and electrolytes.

Top tip

Maintain fluid levels throughout the day by drinking little and often.

Summary

- **Nutrition has an important effect on your overall performance as a footballer.**

- **A balanced diet will ensure you take in enough nutrients to keep you healthy and fit.**

- **Carbohydrate-rich foods need to be eaten to maintain high energy levels while playing matches and training.**

- **Drink enough fluid to stay hydrated.**

Self-tester

- Name five foods that are high in carbohydrates.
- Approximately what percentage of the daily diet of a footballer should be carbohydrates?
- Drinking a lot of water in one go during exercise is the best way to rehydrate. True or false?

Action plan

List the types of food you eat in a week. Check the list against the foods recommended for a balanced diet and one that is rich in carbohydrates. If you need to alter your diet, consider the types of snacks you should eat, and when you should eat them, as well as eating well for the three main meals of the day.

For more information on nutrition and fitness, we advise you to read *The Official FA Guide to Fitness for Football* by Dr Richard Hawkins.

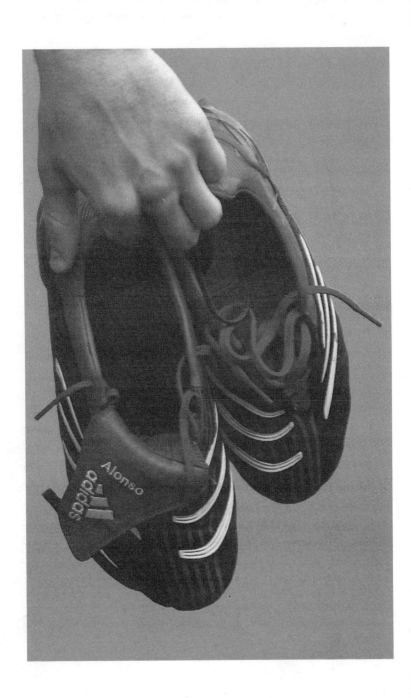

Chapter 4

Choosing your kit

THIS CHAPTER WILL:
- Explain the importance of wearing kit that is appropriate for different conditions.
- Give advice on boot maintenance.
- Give guidance on useful equipment to have for training and playing football.

There has been incredible change in the style and manufacture of football kits in the past 50 years. Compared with the heavy, baggy kit of the 1950s, tops and shorts are now lightweight, breathable and very practical. The invention of synthetic fibres, such as nylon, acrylic and polyester, made a big difference in this respect. Today, kits are constantly changing, largely due to commercial influences on the game.

Statistics

In the nineteenth century players often wore caps, and sometimes even top-hats for matches.

Shirts, shorts and socks

What you choose to play football in is, obviously, down to you. The main consideration is comfort and fit. Make sure that the shorts and top aren't too tight, and wear appropriate layers of clothes for the weather conditions. It is important that you are warm enough in cold weather and cool enough in hot weather, and wearing a few thin layers for training is a good way to regulate your temperature. You must also have layers of clothing, such as a tracksuit and waterproofs, to put on if you are a substitute or are substituted during a match. Sudden changes in body temperature once you stop being active need to be regulated by putting on extra layers for warmth. Also, remember that, in hot weather, dark tops absorb the heat and will make you feel hotter.

Football socks are important items to get right as well. Make sure you choose the correct size, wash them regularly and check that they have no rough areas next to your feet. A problem with your feet caused by a poor pair of socks is unnecessary and could cause you foot injuries severe enough to stop you playing for a few weeks. If your socks cause problems then change them for a new pair.

Top tip

If you find that your socks cause problems for your feet, wear a thin pair of cotton socks beneath your football socks.

Football boots

Colour, make, price and style are probably your main reasons for choosing a particular pair of boots. Try to ask yourself a few more questions about the boots before making your selection:

- Are the football boots comfortable?
- Do the boots fit well, especially in the width, with football socks?

- Are the boots flexible in all directions, including the bottom of the boot?
- Do the boots provide enough protection and support?

Choose your boots wisely and try them on before buying. One difficult decision you need to make concerns the type of studs to use: screw-in, blades or moulded. The main consideration is the condition and type of surface you will be playing on:

Condition of playing surface	Usual types of studs
Soft ground (SG)	Screw-in or blades
Firm ground (FG)	Moulded or short blades
Hard ground (HG)	Rubber studs or Astroturf™

Screw-in studs

Example of screw-in studs

Advantages:

- Studs can be changed if they get worn down, so boots last longer.

- Long and short studs are available for some boots, so they can be changed to match the conditions of the pitch.

- Screw-in studs give excellent grip on soft grounds, enabling you to turn, sprint and stop confidently.

- They are a popular type of boot, so there is plenty of choice of style and brand.

Disadvantages:

- There are usually fewer studs than on moulded boots so pressure points and blisters can occur if they are used on hard pitches.

- If you don't check and tighten the studs regularly you can lose them while playing. Even worse, playing with a loose stud can wear out the screw-thread on the boot so that it can never tighten.

Top tip

Put a little grease or lubricant on the screw to ensure the screw/stud does not rust in place.

Moulded studs

Advantages:

- Moulded boots usually have a large number of studs, so the pressure is more evenly distributed on your foot. This minimizes the chance of blisters.

- The studs are shorter than screw-ins, making them more suitable for firm pitches with grip on the top surface.

- Astroturf™ boots are moulded with pimples or small blades and are excellent for artificial grass on training grounds. They are not suitable for grass unless the ground is very hard.

- The football season is getting longer, with tournaments and footy camps continuing throughout the year. This means that you are likely to play on harder pitches during the summer months.

Disadvantages:

- The studs are usually rubber or nylon, and once they are worn down the boots need replacing.

- On wet surfaces or soft ground they provide very poor grip and will definitely affect your performance.

Statistics

Remember, you will probably run about eight kilometres during a game of football, so your boots are important!

Blades

Advantages:

- There has been a lot of research into the new designs of bladed boots. They claim to provide better turning speed and grip.

- The design means they may be less likely to get stuck in the ground when running.

Example of bladed studs

- Some boots have short and long blades available for different pitch conditions.
- Some blades have replaceable tips so that they can be changed if they become worn or damaged.

Disadvantages:

- If you change from traditional studs to blades they may take a little getting used to as the turning motion is different and does not suit all players.

Uppers

The top of your boots, or uppers, could be leather or synthetic. In some cases the upper will consist of a mixture of the two. Leather can fit comfortably to the shape of the foot, with a good feel to the ball. However, leather can also stretch when wet and go out of shape. Synthetic boots are generally cheaper than leather ones but have improved in recent years. Many now allow the foot to breathe, reducing sweating and making the boot more comfortable to wear. Synthetic uppers are also often used to make a lighter boot.

Choose the boot that is good for you, remembering that comfort is important and so is ball control. The position of the laces now varies, from the traditional top of the foot position to running down the side of the boot. When you try on football boots, decide whether you want the laces off-centre so that they do not get in the way when you strike a ball. Do the boots have a padded tongue that is used to hide the laces, providing a flat surface to strike the ball with? Does the tongue move about or is it secured with velcro or a strap? Also think about the protection that the boot gives your foot. Some lighter boots may offer less protection for the foot but are ideal for fast running as a winger or striker. Other boots may offer good protection but are heavier and may be more suited to defenders, goalkeepers or midfielders.

Looking after your boots

Here are a few tips to keep your boots in good condition. Remember that your boots should not only look good, but also feel good!

- **Undo the laces properly when you take your boots off.**
- **Remove soil by banging the boots together or using a brush, then wipe them with a damp cloth.**
- **If wet, allow the boots to dry before polishing them or giving them a final clean. Don't dry them near a fire or radiator in case the boots crack or lose their shape.**

- Stuffing leather boots with newspaper helps them retain their shape and will help to draw out any moisture from inside the boot.
- Don't play in boots with loose studs, broken studs, mixed studs, or over-tightened studs.
- Don't keep boots in a plastic bag.
- Put your boots on in the dressing room or at the side of the pitch. Walking across car parks or on concrete paths will damage the soles and sharpen the studs or blades.
- Check the boots on a regular basis, looking for any cracks or damage and tightening the studs if necessary.

Equipment list

Make sure you check your bag before you leave for any practices or matches. Here's a checklist of the items you may need to take with you:

- ❏ kit – shorts, top and socks
- ❏ thin inner socks
- ❏ warm-up top/bottoms
- ❏ boots (moulded) for firm ground
- ❏ boots (screw-in/blades) for soft ground
- ❏ boot-bag for muddy boots
- ❏ shin-pads
- ❏ stud key
- ❏ extra pair of laces
- ❏ extra studs for replacements
- ❏ tape or tie-ups for socks
- ❏ towel and shower gel (if shower available)
- ❏ bottle of water/drink
- ❏ first-aid kit – plasters, elasticated bandage, muscle spray etc.
- ❏ small bag for valuables.

For practising the drills in this book, equipment lists are provided for each drill. You will generally need a size 5 ball and a supply of, say, eight cones to mark off boundaries for your practice grids.

Summary

- **Wear kit to suit the weather conditions.**

- **A good boot should give you support, stability, grip and traction.**

- **Choose studs or blades to match the condition of the pitch – use screw-ins or blades for a soft pitch and moulded or short blades for firm pitches.**

- **Keep your boots in good condition to prolong their life.**

- **Always be prepared for a match, checking that your kit is ready and packed to go.**

Self-tester
- Why are dark tops not so good in hot weather?
- Which types of studs are better for soft ground?
- Give two advantages of wearing moulded studs.

Action plan
Check the equipment list and make sure you have all you need for training and for matches. Find a suitable box or bag in which to store all the (clean!) equipment so that you are always organized and prepared each time you play football.

Chapter 5

Warming up and cooling down

THIS CHAPTER WILL:
- Explain the importance of warming up before a match and at the start of training.
- Give an understanding of the importance of cooling down.
- Describe ways to stretch different muscles.

If you go to watch any professional football team playing a match, it is well worth getting to the stadium early to watch the players warming up and stretching. Most teams are out on the pitch 45 minutes before the match, carrying out exercise routines and stretches under the watchful eye of the coach. This is quite a contrast to some local league teams, with players turning up ten minutes before a match and using the run from the changing room to the pitch as their warm-up. Obviously these are two extremes, but this chapter will help to show the importance of a good warm-up and cool down before and after a match, and even during half-time.

The warm-up

The warm-up is designed to prepare a player for any physical activity, both at training and for a match. Your body needs gradually 'waking-up' from a resting state to a state of readiness to train or play. It is important that the warm-up is gradual, building up from easy walking, movement of joints and jogging, through to sprinting and quick turning. Ideally you want a warm-up to match your movements in a game so that similar muscles and joints are prepared for action. In the warm-up, use exercises such as side-strides, sharp turns and jumping, as well as ball control and passing. These exercises will not only prepare muscles and joints, but will also have the advantage of ensuring the effect is on those muscles used for playing football, so helping to prevent injuries. Warming up with a football 'tunes you in' to football skills, preparing you mentally for the game, and gives you the chance get a feel for the playing surface.

Statistics

The recommended time for warming up is between 15 and 25 minutes, completing the warm-up approximately 5–10 minutes before a match.

The main purposes for warming up are:

- to raise body temperature
- to increase muscle temperature
- to reduce muscle tightness
- to help achieve joint mobility
- to prepare the cardiovascular and respiratory systems
- to decrease the risk of injury
- to prepare mentally for physical activity.

The technical bit . . .

The term 'warm-up' implies the key objective of raising body and muscle temperature. As muscles contract they use up energy. Less than a quarter of this energy goes towards producing mechanical work, with the rest of the energy generating heat within the muscle cells. By moving muscles, their performance is improved as their temperature rises. However, this is only one part of improving their performance: raising body temperature by just one degree Celsius is enough to maximize the effect on the active muscles. It has been found that the best way to generate the necessary internal heat is by running.

Mobility and flexibility

Warming up helps you to keep mobile and flexible, through moving your joints and stretching.

* Mobility is the amount of movement your joints will allow.
* Flexibility is the amount of 'stretch' your muscles allow as you move.

Good mobility helps you to turn quickly.

Flexibility exercises increase the stretching potential of the muscles, improving movement. Daily stretching is important, so use the examples on the following page to work out a routine.

Good mobility is essential for sprinting, turning, tackling and shooting. Before any sudden twisting or explosive movements, you need to move your joints in a slow smooth action. Preparing your back and neck is particularly important before any exercise.

Joint rotations

From a balanced, standing position with your arms hanging loosely at your sides, bend, extend, and rotate each of the following joints. Perform eight to ten rotations for each group of joints before moving on to the next group:

- **fingers**
- **wrists**
- **elbows**
- **neck**
- **back and shoulder blades**
- **hips**
- **knees**
- **ankles**
- **feet and toes.**

Work through this sequence of rotations slowly and smoothly, and think about the movements that occur at each joint. Complete the series of joint rotations from fingers to toes in no more than three to four minutes.

Statistics

You begin to lose natural mobility and flexibility from the age of eight, so all players need to know how to work on muscles and joints.

Stretching

Correct stretching of your muscles each day, and especially before training and matches, is important to help avoid injuries and to improve flexibility and performance. Stretching is quite 'static' so it needs to be part of an active warm-up. Common sense and some thought is needed to make the stretching effective:

- Don't over-stretch or put too much strain on your muscles. If there is any pain – stop and find a different position. Stretching shouldn't be painful, just hold a stretch up to a point of tension.

- Don't stretch if your muscles are very cold – warm them up first and also get your joints mobile by rotating and moving wrists, hips, knees etc.

- Start with very gentle stretching, and make each movement slow. Hold a stretch for 10–15 seconds and slowly release, repeating several times.

- Don't 'bounce' into a stretch – you need to control the movement.

- Be systematic so you don't miss out any particular muscle group.

Top tip

Try to develop a daily stretching routine. Spend a few minutes in the morning gently stretching key muscles – it will increase your flexibility and help avoid injuries. Animals such as cats and dogs enjoy a good stretch after waking up – and look at their flexibility!

Try the following stretches for the major muscle groups of the body.

Figure 5.1 **The major muscle groups**

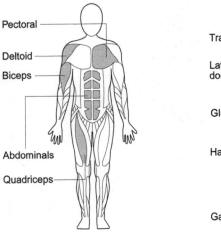
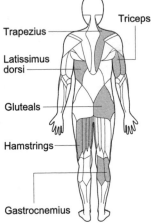

Calf stretch

Facing a wall or partner, step forwards onto a bent left leg. Increasing the weight on your hands, deepen the left leg bend and straighten your right leg back. You should feel the stretch at the top of the calf on the right leg. Try to make the heel of your right leg touch the ground but don't force it. Hold it for ten seconds and repeat three or four times for each leg.

Figure 5.2 **Calf stretch**

Quads stretch

Stand to the side of a wall or use a partner for balance. Gently raise one heel up behind you by grasping the ankle with your hand. Feel the stretch in the quadriceps just above the knees. Repeat with the other leg.

Figure 5.3 **Quads stretch**

Hamstring stretch – standing

Straighten one leg in front of you and slightly bend the other leg. Place both hands on the thigh of your bent leg and sit back gently. Don't bounce. Hold it for 10–15 seconds and then change legs.

Figure 5.4 **Hamstring stretch – standing**

Hamstring stretch – lying down

Lie on your back with your legs out flat. With your hands holding behind your left knee, raise your leg at the hip, with the knee still bent at 90 degrees. Hold this position and then slowly raise your leg at the knee joint until a stretch can be felt in the hamstring muscles. Relax and repeat three or four times for each leg.

Figure 5.5 **Hamstring stretch – lying down**

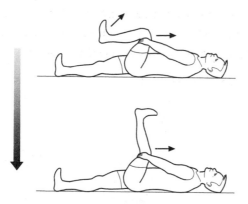

Gluteal stretch

Sit on the ground with knees pointing skywards. Cross your left leg over your right so it is resting behind the knee. Gently pull the crossed leg towards your chest with the help of the other leg, but don't pull too far. Repeat for other leg.

Figure 5.6 **Gluteal stretch**

Groin inward stretch

Sit on the floor with your knees bent and lean back on your hands. Slowly push one leg in and downward until you feel a little strain on your thigh. Hold it for 5–10 seconds, release and repeat four times on each leg.

Figure 5.7 **Groin inward stretch**

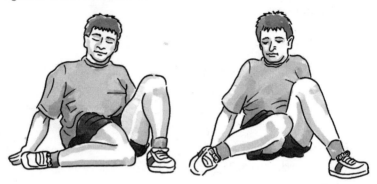

Groin outward stretch

Stand with legs wide apart and weight even, knees slightly bent and hands on hips. Increase the bend in one leg and straighten the other by sliding it out so you take a sideways lunge. Don't bounce, and don't bend the knee of the bent leg beyond the foot position.

Figure 5.8 **Groin outward stretch**

Back stretch

Lie on your back and bring in your hips and knees until your knees touch your chest. Put your hands on your knees and gently pull them towards your chest, lifting your hips slightly. Lift your head carefully and slowly off the ground until you feel a slight stretch in your back.

Figure 5.9 **Back stretch**

Side stretch

Stand upright and balanced. Reach your left hand up and over your head, bending slowly to your right. Slide your right hand down your right leg as you bend. Keep your hips still and your weight evenly balanced as you bend. Don't bounce. Repeat this stretch for the other side.

Figure 5.10 **Side stretch**

Stomach stretch

Lie on your back with your arms stretched up over your head on the ground. Stretch as far as you can, with your toes pointed forwards and fingers reaching back. Hold the stretch for 30 seconds.

Figure 5.11 **Stomach stretch**

Fast-feet and speed

Speed is crucial in football, whether it's for a quick, heart-pumping five-metre sprint, or a lung-gasping 50-metre break. In a race for the ball between a defender and a striker, pace makes all the difference between winning and losing possession. This is why most teams include some 'fast-feet' and speed drills in the warm-up. They tune you in for the match, improving coordination and speed and preparing your brain and nerves for the fast movements to come in the match.

As part of your warm-up, try to include five to ten minutes of drills involving quick foot movements and sprinting over small distances. Try the following drills and make up some of your own.

On the spot

Jog on the spot and then sprint hard on the spot, pumping your arms for five seconds. Relax into a jog and repeat. Continue this, but vary the fast-feet movement:

- move in a 'figure of 8' on the spot
- sprint and end with a header
- sprint with knees up.

Taps

Place two footballs ten metres apart. Sprint from one football to the other. When you reach a football, hop quickly from foot to foot, tapping the top of the ball with alternate feet. Repeat this for ten sprints. Vary the action at each football:

- pass the ball quickly from side to side
- bend the leg and touch the top of the ball with alternate knees.

Zig-zag

Set up two rows of five cones, hurdles, footballs or any markers, about three metres apart. Run to the first marker on the right-hand side and place your right foot over it. Push off from this foot and accelerate across to the first marker on the left row. Continue with the zig-zag pathway, moving sideways quickly and pushing off to change direction.

Shuttles

Place four markers in a row, each three metres apart. Make a start-line, three metres in front of the first marker. Sprint to each marker in any order, touching them with one hand and returning to the start-line each time.

A warm-up programme

Before each match and at the start of training, your coach is likely to plan a 15–20 minute programme for warming up, which includes stretching. It is always a good idea to stretch once your muscles have warmed up a little, after an initial jog. Below is an outline of a programme that can be adapted for your use before a match:

Activities	Duration/distance
1. Jog – very easy pace across pitch and back twice.	4 × 50 metres
2. Joint rotations – slow circular movement of all joints: ankles, knees, hips, wrists, elbows, shoulders. Gentle neck and back movements.	3 minutes
3. Jog – cruising pace across pitch and back twice. Try to include: • normal run • side-strides • running backwards • cross-steps during run.	4 × 50 metres
4. Stretching – light stretching (quads, hamstrings, groin, back) as well as any specific stretches you feel help.	5 minutes
5. Fast-feet drills – on the spot	2 minutes
6. Speed drills – 10-metre course: • run 3 metres, decelerate to end, then run back hard – short strides • sideways run along start-line then sprint forward 10 metres • jump twice at start then sprint forward 10 metres.	3 minutes
7. Ball work in pairs – 15–25 ball touches per player each minute.	5 minutes

Warming down

Cooling or warming down is seen as essential in many other sports such as athletics, swimming and cycling, but it is only in recent years that it has become part of the routine after football matches. It is often easier to fit in a warm-down after training than after a match because all the players are still wound up in the emotions of the game they have just played. However, warming down after a match should be part of your routine if you want to look after your body.

The most important thing is that a warm-down is active but gentle. You are aiming to return your heart rate and respiration gradually back to normal, and to allow the waste products (lactic acid) from the muscles to be reabsorbed. If you cool down too quickly at the end of a match or training, particularly if you have been working very hard, you are more likely to suffer from muscle stiffness caused by a build-up of lactic acid. The graph in Figure 5.12 shows the importance of an active warm-down.

Figure 5.12 **Levels of lactic acid after activity (Bangsbo1994)**
Source: *Fitness Training in Football – A Scientific Approach*, Jens Bangsbo
(Ho & Storm) (1994)

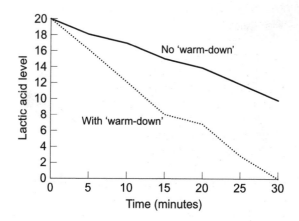

Immediately after a match, take a few minutes' rest. Your coach may wish to talk to you and this is when you will share the experience of the match with your team-mates. It is important that you take in fluids to start rehydration at this stage. The best form of warm-down is jogging at an easy pace for several minutes, going down to a walk. Ten minutes' warm-down is enough to have a positive effect.

Gentle stretching can also be part of the warm-down. It helps bring your body back towards a state of rest and recovery and allows you to focus on relaxing and lengthening the muscles that you have put under stress during the match or training session.

Top tip

Warm down after each match or training session with a gentle jog and stretch. Not only will it ease any muscle aches, but it has also been shown to improve your sleep in the immediate nights that follow.

Summary

- **Warming up and warming down need to be part of your routine before and after matches and training.**

- **Stretching is important to maximize performance and reduce the risk of injury.**

- **Make stretching and joint movement part of a daily routine.**

Self-tester

- Give three reasons for warming up before a match.
- Describe a stretch for your hamstring.
- Why are 'fast-feet' exercises useful as part of the warm-up before a match?

Action plan

Plan a warm-up routine for yourself before a match or training session. Think about a balance of exercises for the different parts of your body. Get into the habit of stretching muscles and moving joints as a routine each day.

For more information on warming up and cooling down, we advise you to read *The Official FA Guide to Fitness for Football* by Dr Richard Hawkins.

Chapter 6

Dealing with injuries

THIS CHAPTER WILL:
- Describe the different sorts of injuries that you may be unlucky enough to get as a footballer.
- Outline ways to help you prevent injuries.
- Explain the basic treatments that are needed for different injuries.

Football is a high-energy body-contact sport, so at some stage in your football career you will get an injury. Don't let this put you off though! The more informed you are about the different types of possible injuries and the ways to avoid and treat them, the more chance you have of getting through each season with fewer injury problems.

Statistics

A total of more than 3,000 injuries are suffered each season by the 2,500 or so professionals in the Premier League and Football League. Each injury keeps a player out of the game for an average of four matches.

The information in this chapter is only for guidance and general interest. If you are concerned about any injuries you have, and certainly if the injury is serious, you must seek medical advice from your doctor or visit a hospital.

Types of injury

There are two different types of sporting injury: **chronic** and **acute**. The causes for these make each distinctive.

Chronic injuries

These are caused by continuous stress on a particular part of the body over a long period of time. Examples for other sports include tennis elbow or golfer's elbow. There are fewer chronic injuries involved with football, but if you overuse a particular part of the body for too long you may develop a chronic injury. A possible problem from running long distances in training is an injury called 'shin splints'. Symptoms include:

- **tenderness on the inside of the shin**
- **lower leg pain**
- **possible swelling**
- **pain when the foot is bent downwards**
- **a slight redness to the shin.**

If you suffer from this, the main thing to do is rest. You can apply ice in the early stages when it is very painful, but the sooner you rest the sooner it will heal. To prevent chronic injuries, train carefully, rest between training sessions, wear good footwear and improve your technique.

Acute injuries

These are caused by a sudden stress on the body and are more common than chronic injuries in football. They can include bone fractures, pulled muscles, concussion or bruising. It is useful to separate these types of injuries into soft-tissue and hard-tissue injuries.

Soft-tissue injuries

These include:

- open injuries where the skin is broken, such as cuts, grazes and blisters
- closed injuries that happen beneath the skin, including:
  - bruises – blood vessels are damaged
  - strains – pulled muscles and tendons from torn tissue
  - sprains – ligaments stretched or torn at a joint, such as an ankle
  - dislocation – bone pulled out of its normal position at a joint
  - torn cartilage – damage to the cartilage around a joint such as the knee.

Statistics

The commonest type of injury in football, by a long way, is muscle strain. This accounts for about one-third of all injuries.

Hard-tissue injuries

These injuries are bone fractures. They could be cracks in the bone, or an actual break. With a fractured bone there is likely to be bruising and swelling, as well as a great deal of pain because of the damaged nerves inside the bone.

Treating injuries

The majority of the injuries you will get through playing football will be minor soft-tissue injuries, such as sprains, strains and bruises. The RICE method is a good way to treat these:

R   Rest   → stop immediately and rest the injury.

I   Ice   → apply ice to the injury to make the blood vessels contract and reduce swelling.

C   Compression   → put on a bandage (not too tight) to help reduce swelling.

E   Elevation   → raise the injury to reduce the flow of blood.

Anything more serious than a minor soft-tissue injury will need proper medical attention. This includes any fracture, dislocation or torn cartilage, or any injury to the head.

Looking after your feet

Feet are obviously a key part of the body when playing football, and yet foot-care advice is largely ignored by many footballers. Infections and painful problems can result if simple advice isn't followed, possibly preventing you from training and playing.

Blisters

Blisters are layers of the outer surface of the skin separated from one another, caused by twisting or friction on the feet. The empty space between the separated skin layers is often filled with fluid. If this fluid contains blood, this signifies a deeper blister that will need treatment to stop infection.

Prevention

To help prevent blisters:

- ensure correctly fitting footwear
- introduce the wearing of new footwear slowly
- wet and 'stretch' areas of footwear that may cause friction
- wear thin cotton socks, perhaps sweat-absorbent ones, under football socks
- try applying Vaseline or other similar 'second skins' on areas of the foot liable to friction.

Treatment

To treat blisters:

- clean the area with antiseptic cream or lotion
- apply cotton-backed tape and a large foam pad over the area, with a hole cut to the size of the blister.

Calluses

These are caused by excessive friction and pressure, resulting in a thickening of the skin. They are tender and painful to touch.

Prevention

To help prevent calluses:

- ensure correctly fitting footwear
- wear thin cotton socks, perhaps sweat-absorbent ones, under football socks
- make sure you don't have a problem with the alignment of your foot – see a doctor or podiatrist to check this.

Treatment

To treat calluses:

- visit a podiatrist or chiropodist who will trim the calluses, so relieving the pressure
- consider changing your footwear to give a better fit
- correct your foot alignment if this is diagnosed as a problem.

Athlete's foot

This is caused by a fungus and can spread very quickly. This is particularly the case if players walk around barefoot in changing rooms with contaminated floors. It commonly occurs between the toes where the skin becomes white and scaly. It is usually itchy and you may feel a burning sensation.

Prevention

To help prevent athlete's foot:

- wear flip-flops in changing rooms and shower areas
- use footbaths
- dry between your toes after washing and applying talcum powder if necessary
- don't share towels or socks with other players.

Treatment

To treat athlete's foot:

- consult a doctor or pharmacist
- use the prescribed anti-fungal cream, lotion or powder regularly until the infection goes
- keep the toes clean, dry and out in the air during this period.

Ingrowing toenail

Problems may occur if you cut your nails too short, or cut down into each corner. This may cause a red swelling of the skin and a discharge from the nail bed around the edge of the nail. In extreme cases you may get an ingrown toenail, when the nail, or a ragged nail spike, grows down into the skin at the side of the nail.

Prevention

To help prevent ingrowing toenails:

- **ensure correctly fitting footwear**
- **keep your nails cut even and short, but not too short**
- **don't cut down into the corners of your nails**
- **use a file to smooth the edges of the nail.**

Treatment

If the area around the nail is painful, inflamed and red or has a discharge of fluid, then consult a doctor, podiatrist or chiropodist.

Top tip

One of the main causes of foot problems, including ingrowing toenails, blisters and calluses, are badly fitting shoes, boots or trainers. Choose your footwear carefully, for comfort, not brand, making sure that they are not too tight or too loose.

Getting cramp and stitch

Cramp

Some people suffer with this more than others, but if you've ever had cramp during a match you'll know it is very painful and makes it almost impossible to continue playing. Your muscle contracts or spasms, with a feeling as if it has 'locked up'. Fortunately, it usually goes off after a while, but if you suffer with cramp consistently it may be a good idea to consult your doctor about it. Why it happens is still partly unknown and based on different theories. It is probably caused by a number of factors including:

- dehydration
- overheating
- a lack of blood flowing to the muscles
- a lack of salt minerals in the blood
- a build-up of lactic acid in the muscles.

Prevention

To help prevent cramp:

- drink plenty of fluids
- eat a diet that is suitable for a footballer (see pages 45–48)
- warm up and stretch well before the match (see pages 65–77)
- rehydrate with fluid at half-time.

Treatment

To treat cramp:

- take the weight off the affected muscle
- carefully stretch the muscle and hold it in a stretched position
- massage the muscle gently to relax it and get the blood flowing
- drink an isotonic drink to make up for the salt mineral loss.

Stitch

Stitches are likely to be caused by a muscle cramp of the diaphragm – the muscle that helps us breathe. When we inhale we move the diaphragm down, when we exhale (breathe out) it moves up. The diaphragm is positioned between the chest cavity and the abdominal cavity, with the internal organs in the abdomen connected to the diaphragm. During running these organs are bounced around and pull down on the diaphragm as we exhale, causing a stitch. Interestingly most people get a stitch on the right side which is where the largest organ, the liver, is located.

Prevention

To help prevent stitch:

* breathe deeply when running
* try to relax your chest and stomach.

Treatment

To treat stitch:

* stop exercising for a short while
* take deep breaths
* breathe out slowly.

Top tip

If you get a stitch while running, try breathing out as your left foot hits the ground. The organs on your left side are smaller than on the right side so this may reduce the effect of a stitch.

Preventing injuries

Many minor injuries sustained during a football match or training session can be avoided. This is particularly true for foot problems.

Before the game

Before any match or training session, make sure you:

* check that your feet are in good condition, with nails cut and any blisters or other problems treated
* take off watches and jewellery etc.
* check that the area you are practising or playing on is free from glass and stones

- warm up correctly, preparing your muscles and joints
- wear comfortable, well-fitting trainers or boots
- wear a thin pair of cotton socks under your football socks
- check that the stud length suits the condition of the pitch
- use a good pair of shin-pads.

During the game

Make sure you:

- use the correct technique for passing, tackling, heading and shooting
- keep warmed up if you are a substitute
- keep your fluid levels up by having a drink at half-time.

After the game

Be sure to:

- cool down properly
- rest properly to give yourself good recovery time before playing again.

Statistics

Approximately one-third of injuries are sustained during training, while the remaining two-thirds occur during matches.

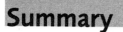

Summary

- Chronic injuries are caused by overuse over time. Acute injuries are more common in football and are caused by sudden stress.

- Most acute injuries in football are minor soft-tissue injuries, such as bruising, strains and sprains. Hard-tissue injuries are bone fractures.

- The RICE method is a good way to treat minor soft-tissue injuries.

- Look after your feet!

- Try to prevent injuries and problems before they occur.

Self-tester

- Give an example of a chronic sporting injury.
- What does RICE stand for?
- What are the best ways to prevent blisters?
- Describe the probable cause of a stitch.

Action plan

List the injuries and problems, however minor, that you have had in the past few years through playing football. For each injury write down possible ways these could have been avoided. Use this to give yourself a checklist of things to do to help prevent or limit injuries in the future.

Part 3

Improving your game

Chapter 7

Football fundamentals

THIS CHAPTER WILL:
- Outline some of the basic skills required by all young footballers, irrespective of what position they are playing in.
- Give technique tips that will help players understand these basic skills.

There are certain basic skills that all footballers need to develop and practise. Football is a team game, with passing the ball an essential part of keeping the ball and developing attacking play. All players need to pass the ball competently and confidently. Controlling the ball from a pass is another basic skill that can be practised. Having a good first touch when receiving the ball looks an effortless skill from top professionals, but it requires excellent technique and great concentration. Other basic skills needed by all players include tackling, shooting and running with the ball. You, as a defender, need to practise the techniques needed for these skills, to help you become a good all-round team player.

Passing

Passing is the most frequently used technique in the game of football. Coaches will often say 'if you can't pass the ball you can't play', which is why passing is one of football's fundamentals. Without the ability to pass the ball accurately and precisely your team will struggle to keep possession and build up attempts on goal.

Statistic

The player in the England squad who has the highest pass completion rate is Gary Neville, who sees 81 per cent of his passes completed.

Gary Neville is a master of passing the ball.

A good player will have a wide range of passing techniques, using different parts of the foot surface. These include:

- the inside of the foot
- the outside of the foot

- the instep of the foot
- the toe
- the sole of the foot
- the heel of the foot.

You will also need to consider the different passing options:

- Do you need to make a short pass?
- Does the ball need to travel a long distance?
- Do you want to pass in the air or on the ground?

These decisions help you to choose the type of pass to make. You also need to consider the following important elements:

- whether to disguise the pass
- the speed or weight of the pass
- the timing of the pass
- the accuracy of the pass.

When a player can effectively and regularly deliver on these elements, they will be considered a good passer of the ball for their team.

Top tip

A good pass is one that arrives just in front of the receiver so they can take the ball without breaking stride and move up field to build their team's attempt on goal – which is an attacking principle of play and the main objective of being in possession.

Although there are many passing techniques that you can practise, this section considers three of the most common passes used in the modern game:

- the push pass
- the low driven pass
- the lofted pass.

The push pass

The push pass is the most commonly used pass at all levels of football. For passes up to approximately 25 metres, the push pass is also the most accurate.

The technique

You should approach the ball at a slight angle, with your non-kicking foot placed alongside the ball. Be careful not to get too close as this will prevent you from swinging your kicking leg freely. The ankle of the passing foot should be kept firm. The ball is then passed using the inside of your kicking foot, making contact through the middle of the ball. For accuracy you should follow through in the same direction as the target of the pass. At all times the head remains steady with eyes fixed on the ball.

A push pass is the most accurate type of pass.

The low driven pass

A common pass for footballers to master is the low driven pass. It allows players to pass the ball over longer distances and also at a greater pace, so that the ball reaches the receiver in a shorter period of time.

The technique

The technique is similar to the push pass, but with modifications at the point of striking the ball. You should approach the ball at a slight angle, with your non-kicking foot placed alongside the ball. For this pass, however, the standing foot needs to be slightly in front of the ball. Be careful not to get too close, as this will prevent you from swinging your kicking foot freely through the ball. Your passing foot ankle should be firm.

The ball is then passed with the kicking foot making contact through the middle of the ball. The kicking foot needs to fully extend down so that the photo looks like it's been made using the inside of the foot. Once again,

A low driven pass will travel a greater distance.

the follow-through is important and should follow the line of the intended target. At all times the head remains steady, with eyes fixed on the ball.

The lofted pass

When players are choosing their passing options, one thing they will need to consider is whether to pass the ball on the ground or in the air. If the opposition have players in between the passer and the team-mate being passed to, then one option is to try the lofted pass. This will take the ball over the head of the defending player and hopefully into the path of the attacker.

The technique

You approach the ball at a slight angle and plant your standing foot alongside the ball, but this time slightly behind the ball. Your last stride into the ball will be longer than previous strides. This allows you to increase the length of the back-swing on your kicking foot. You must not plant your standing foot too close to the ball or it will interfere with

A lofted pass will take the ball over the head of the defending player.

swinging your kicking leg freely. Similar to the low driven pass, the point of contact with the ball is made through the laces (the instep) of the boot. However, with this particular pass the contact is made with the underside of the ball. Although it is still important to keep the head steady with eyes fixed on the ball, the body position should be slightly leaning back. The length of the back-swing of the kicking foot and the pace of the follow-through increases the distance of the pass. For accuracy, it is important that the follow-through is in line with the intended target.

Top tip

Remember to practise your techniques using both feet, not just the foot you prefer.

Ball control

If you watch top players you will soon notice how comfortable they are receiving the ball. They are concerned about what they are going to do next, rather than about receiving the ball. Ball control is another football fundamental and something all good players will have spent hours practising on the training ground. You can gain or lose vital seconds depending on how good you are at controlling the ball. As soon as the ball is under control, players quickly consider what to do next. Do they:

- look to run with the ball?
- look to dribble?
- try to shoot?
- try to pass the ball to a team-mate? (This is the most common option.)

So you need to practise getting the ball quickly under control so that you can keep possession of the ball for your team and develop the attacking play. There are four surfaces of the body that you can use to control the ball:

- the feet
- the chest
- the thigh
- the head.

For the purposes of this chapter we will concentrate on the basic techniques for controlling the ball with the feet, thighs and chest.

Top tip

Players should look to play their first touch away from their body and into a position that will allow them to immediately consider their options – whether to run with ball, dribble, shoot or pass, on their second touch.

Whatever surface is chosen to control the ball, there are real advantages of playing the ball out and in front of the body with the first touch. By doing this:

- you will gain time to consider options, as the ball is not stuck under the foot
- you will improve your vision for passing/shooting options as your head is likely to be up
- your accuracy will be improved as a vital gap is created between your feet and the ball to help effective technique.

There are two basic types of ball control, the **cushion control** and the **wedge control**. Both can be used by all the different surfaces, though the techniques in this chapter concentrate on the following:

- cushion control using the inside of the foot
- cushion control using the top of the foot
- cushion control using the thigh

- cushion control using the chest
- wedge control using the feet.

Cushion control using the inside of the foot
The technique

It is important to be well balanced when you are receiving the ball, so you must move into the line of the ball as early as possible. This gives you less chance of being caught off balance. Decide which foot you will be controlling the ball with and watch the ball onto the side of your foot (keep your eye on the ball at all times). As the ball meets your foot, immediately pull back or withdraw the inside of the foot. This will provide a cushioning effect and should leave the ball close to your foot but slightly ahead of you, so you can choose your next option with your second touch.

If you do not withdraw on impact, the ball is likely to bounce away from you and into the path of the opposition. The head should remain still throughout, with eyes fixed on the ball.

Cushion control using the inside of the foot

Cushion control using the top of the foot

The technique

Once again it is important to be well balanced when you receive the ball. For this reason there are advantages to getting into line with the ball as early as possible so you are not stretching for the ball. Decide which foot you will be controlling the ball with and watch the ball onto the foot. For this technique it is likely to be your preferred kicking foot, as it is a slightly more difficult technique than using the inside of the foot.

As the ball meets your foot, on the laces of your boot, immediately withdraw or pull back your foot. You should see the ball cushioned and resting just in front of you. If the ball is a comfortable distance from your body then your second touch can be a pass, shot or dribble. The head should remain still throughout the practice with eyes fixed on the ball.

Cushion control using the top of the foot

Cushion control using the thigh

The technique

With all the ball control techniques it is important to be well balanced and composed as you receive the ball. The best chance of this happening is to get in line with the ball as quickly as possible. Depending on the flight of the ball and your positioning, you will need to select which thigh you are going to use to control the ball. After offering your thigh to the ball, as soon as contact is made, withdraw your leg. This should provide the cushioning effect for the ball to rest close to your feet, but just far enough away from you so your next touch can be a pass, dribble or shot. Keep your head still throughout with your eyes fixed on the ball. The ball will bounce away from you if you do not withdraw your thigh on impact.

Cushion control using the thigh

Cushion control using the chest

The technique

This technique is very similar to the previous three techniques, with the same principles applying. Be well balanced when receiving the ball. Get in line with the ball as quickly as possible and watch the ball onto the chest, with your head remaining steady. As the ball makes impact with your chest try to withdraw the surface by leaning back slightly. This will see the ball bounce up a little, but will provide the cushioning impact which will allow the ball to drop down near your feet to let you play your second touch. In order to lean back, you will need to bend your knees. Spreading your arms out slightly may help with balance and can also help to shield the ball if marked by a defender.

Cushion control using the chest

Wedge control using the feet

The technique

This is a slightly more difficult technique to master than cushion control. With cushion control you withdraw or pull back the surface on impact with the ball. The wedge control is the opposite movement: immediately on impact you redirect the ball away from your body and into the available space. This technique of controlling the ball is more likely to be used if you do not have so much time to receive the ball.

As with the cushion control, it is important to be well balanced when you are receiving the ball, so you must move into the line of the ball as early as possible. Decide which foot you will be controlling the ball with and watch the ball onto your foot. You can use either the inside or outside of the foot for the first touch. As the ball meets your foot, immediately jab or push down so that the ball does not go too far away from you, but is played away into space.

Receiving and turning

This is a basic skill for any developing player – to have the ability to turn with the ball as you receive it. Whenever a ball is played to you, one of the options available to you is to turn. Your body position is vital for this, so that you are looking to turn as you receive the ball.

Receiving the ball with an open body position

The earlier a young player is able to turn with the ball and look to receive the ball with an open body position, the quicker their game will develop. Receiving the ball this way allows play to be switched in a single movement. You only need to watch the top players to see how this is an automatic way for them to receive the ball. They are always checking behind them so that, if the opponent makes it difficult to turn, they can look to shield the ball or pass. If space and time permit, players should look to receive the ball with an open body position. This will allow them not only to switch play but also see the whole pitch to help them decide what to do next.

The technique

As the ball is being passed to you, decide which foot you are going to receive the ball with. If you are receiving the ball with your right foot, then your left foot acts as an anchor. As the ball impacts onto your right foot and you cushion the impact of the ball, you should already be half turned to your right as you take the pace off the ball.

The ball should carry on at a slower pace, allowing you to complete your outward body turn quickly. The ball should still be under control while you face a new direction, ready to switch play or pass the ball down the channel. This technique is particularly useful for full-backs when they are receiving the ball from goalkeepers and need to look for passes into wide midfielders.

> ## Top tip
>
> The secret to receiving and turning is to take most of the pace off
> the ball and turn at the same time to follow it. Simple, but like all
> techniques it needs practising on the training ground.

Tackling

Dispossessing your opponent is the primary aim of tackling and if you
can emerge with the ball then you really have put your team in a strong
position. However, if you have prevented your opponent from making
progress then you have still done your job.

Statistic

Rio Ferdinand, although a defender, only averages a tackle
every 43 minutes. However, playing as a sweeper will often
involve him intercepting and covering other defenders.

Tackling is a football fundamental. All players, no matter what position
they play in, must have the technical ability to tackle and defend for their
team. As a defender you will be the last line of defence. Being able to
'jockey' and make tackles when needed will win matches for your team.
With players in possession seeming to have more and more protection
from referees, it is extremely important that you time your tackle
correctly and fairly. The chances of being booked or sent off are greater
now than they have ever been.

We will now look at the techniques associated with:

- timing the tackle
- the block tackle
- the slide tackle.

Top tip

Be patient – only tackle if you are sure you can win the ball. After committing to the tackle you could be left stranded with your opponent through on goal. Any player who charges into tackles without thinking is a liability to their team.

Principles of tackling

A defender's first task is to delay the attacker by 'jockeying' – keeping your body between the attacker and the goal, backing off slightly as the attacker moves forward and waiting for the right moment to tackle. This delaying tactic gives other players in your team the time to get back to defend.

In preparation you should adopt the 'ready stance', with knees bent, facing the opponent at an angle and watching the ball, not the movements of the player.

You need to be fairly close to the player on the ball. If the time is right to make the tackle, this will allow you to get all your strength and weight behind the ball in an attempt to win it. Your ankle and knee should be locked solidly, which will maintain strength and reduce injury.

You must try to get your foot behind the back of the ball when making the challenge. This way you will get more force behind the ball and reduce the chance of injuring your opponent with an 'over the top' tackle, which could see a player being seriously injured.

Quote | To be a good defender you need to like defending, like challenges, like tackling.'
Steve McClaren

'Jockeying' is part of a defender's game.

Timing of the tackle

Timing a tackle is an art in itself. As a defender you must assess your options as quickly as possible in order to help you gain an advantage.

The technique

If your opponent does not have the ball under control and has their head down, this may be your signal to make the tackle. If they have the ball under control and are looking up, weighing up their options, then it may be best to be cautious and patient and wait for the right time to tackle.

It is good practice to wait until your opponent pushes the ball out of their feet before making your challenge. When this happens the ball is furthest away from their body and not under direct control. When you feel the time is right to make the tackle try to stay on your feet and not go to ground.

The block tackle

This is a very common tackle in the modern game. It is important to practise good technique.

The technique

You need to be reasonably close to the player in possession. When the time is right to make the tackle, the non-kicking foot is placed alongside the ball and the ankle joint and the knee of the tackling leg must be firm and locked. Your knees should be slightly bent which lowers the centre of gravity and makes a more powerful and compact body shape.

The block tackle is a common tackle.

The ideal position for your head and upper body is over the ball. Some players may choose to make a fist with their hands, which tightens their upper body. The actual tackle is made with the kicking foot making contact through the middle and back of the ball. Although every player can practise the technique of tackling, success often comes down to a positive and aggressive attitude.

The slide tackle

It is wise to use the slide tackle only as a last resort because it involves you going to ground and takes you out of the game for a short time. After making the slide tackle, you should try to get back on your feet as quickly as possible. A slide tackle is one of the more difficult defensive skills to learn, though when done effectively and for good purpose it can add defensive qualities to you and your team.

The slide tackle should be used as a last resort.

The technique

With this particular tackle you approach the player with the ball from a side-on position. Keep your eye on the ball rather than on your opponent. As you turn sideways into the tackle, the arm nearest the opponent should be extended and reach for the ground to take your upper body weight as you slide to the ground.

The leg closest to the ball and player should be allowed to collapse to enable you to get to the ground quickly. While on the ground your other leg should be extended to use a sweeping action to win the ball.

If you are unable to keep possession of the ball, then you should try to redirect the ball away from the player. After performing this tackle you must try to get back on your feet as quickly as possible, using your inside arm to lever yourself up.

Shooting

Statistic

A team that has ten shots on target is likely to win a match.

There is a saying in football: 'never pass when you can shoot'. However, knowing when to shoot requires a split-second decision. Coaches will often encourage you to shoot if you get a chance or even a half chance. This relies on the player having confidence and a positive attitude towards shooting at goal.

Shooting is the most important aspect of attacking play and therefore the requirement on players to practise their shooting technique is fundamental to them becoming a better player.

It is important for you as a defender to be able to take shooting opportunities when they arise. It is not just the strikers that score goals, so work on your shooting technique when you can.

Top tip

You will miss more than you score when taking shots on goal, but do remain positive about taking shots whenever the opportunity arises. However, you must remember to pass to a team-mate if they are in a better position to score.

Although there are many different techniques associated with shooting we will look at two of the most common types:

- shooting with the inside of the foot
- the low driven shot.

Principles of shooting

- It is better to shoot wide than high, because a shot going wide may still have some chance of being deflected into the goal.
- Accuracy is more important than power, as a powerful shot off target merely presents the opposition with a goal kick.
- A low shot has more potential of beating the goalkeeper than a high shot, which goalkeepers find easier to save.
- Shots going away from a goalkeeper, towards the far post are usually more difficult to save than shots to the near post. They also have more chance of coming into the path of another striker if the goalkeeper is unable to hold onto the shot.

Shooting with the inside of the foot

This particular shooting technique supports the idea that it is more important to be accurate than powerful, though both are ideal. Many players who shoot with the inside of the foot are at relatively close range as it is considered to be the most accurate technique. They are often 'picking their spot' and placing the ball past the keeper towards one corner of the net.

The technique

This is very similar technique to the push pass though with a little more power. You should approach the ball from a slight angle and place your kicking foot alongside the ball. Your head remains steady and your eyes should be fixed on the ball. If you have time, take a quick look up and then back at the ball just before shooting to assess the position of the goalkeeper and the goal.

Your shooting leg is taken back and contact is made with the ball through the inside of the foot coming into contact with the mid-line of the ball. The follow-through is in the direction of the goal.

Shooting with the inside of the foot is considered to be the most accurate technique.

The low driven shot

Players who decide to shoot with the low driven shot technique are usually intent on gaining power as well as accuracy. They are also likely to have a positive mental attitude towards shooting. It is a common technique used when there is an opportunity to shoot from outside the penalty area, where power is needed to beat the goalkeeper.

The technique

This particular technique is almost identical to the low driven pass technique, but obviously with more power. The approach is from a slight angle, with the non-kicking foot alongside and slightly in front of the ball. Your kicking foot should be fully extended as it makes contact with the back of the ball, which is struck with the laces of the boot. The follow-through takes place through the centre of the ball and in line with the intended target.

Shooting using the low driven shot

Quote | 'You mustn't be afraid to miss.'
Mark Hughes

Running with the ball

The technical ability to run confidently with the ball at their feet makes the difference between a good player and an average one. Practising this technique, once again, provides a player with a fundamental skill for playing the game.

A combination of strength and speed is required if you want to take the ball forward at your feet, beat defenders and get into the opposition's defensive third. It is a skill that benefits all players in a team. There is no better sight in the game than an accomplished defender or midfielder breaking forward with the ball to be part of an attack, or a striker turning with the ball and running at a defence.

The technique

You should aim to keep the ball approximately one to two metres in front of you and use your arms to assist you with your running style and balance. Use the outside of your foot, or your instep (laces) to push the ball in front of you.

Keep you head up so that you can see what is going on around you. Every few strides you may need to glance down to see the position of the ball. Try to increase your speed, using good arm and leg action while still keeping control of the ball.

Top tip

Don't let a player chasing you affect your concentration. If you get a chance, try to run across and in front of them. This may see them committing a foul on you as they try to track back.

Summary

- Defenders need to be confident passers of the ball, using a variety of techniques to keep the ball in possession.

- When receiving the ball be ready to turn and use cushion or wedge control techniques to keep the ball.

- Tackling is a basic skill for all players, with defenders being the last line of defence.

- Shooting is a fundamental skill for attacking football, with practice needed to master the techniques.

- All players need to be confident with the ball at their feet, running in space or in front of opposition players.

Self-tester

- Describe the technique used for a push pass.
- Is your body position leaning forward or back for a lofted pass?
- What is the purpose of an open body position when receiving a pass?
- Describe the basic technique of a block tackle.

Action plan

Practise these fundamental skills each week so that you increase your confidence in each of these aspects of play.

Chapter 8

Individual practice drills for defenders

THIS CHAPTER WILL:
- Help you to develop the skills and techniques required to become an effective defender.
- Provide drills and practices you can work on, either on your own or with a team-mate.

The previous chapter highlighted the basic skills of passing, ball control when receiving the ball, tackling, shooting and running with the ball that all footballers need. Although these skills and techniques are fundamental for the developing player, there are also some specific individual skills and techniques required for the position of defender.

Almost all of the technical skills for this position can be improved with practice. Look back at page 28 in Chapter 1 to remind yourself of the key attributes of a good defender.

Quote | 'Who is the best defender in the Premiership at the moment? John Terry – he is a stopper, a leader and takes pride in the job he does.'
David Moyes

John Terry is one of the best defenders in the game.

This chapter provides some examples of drills and practices that you can try on your own or with another team-mate to improve the fundamental skills and the more specific skills and techniques for the defender. The majority of the practices need another person to work with, although if you are on your own some of the practices can be adapted by using a rebound wall. If you are using a wall, please make sure it has a smooth finish, and that it is in a safe area, not near to a road or windows.

Passing

Good players and good teams can keep possession of the ball because they have a wide range of passing techniques and the ability to know where to pass, what type of pass to use and when to pass. As mentioned in the previous chapter there are many different types of pass which can be made in the modern game. Different parts of the foot and the body can be used to provide both short and long passes. The high level of ability often seen when watching top players is only achieved as a result of many hours on the training pitch practising existing and new techniques.

Here, we will highlight the techniques and suitable drills to help you develop the following range of passes:

- **push pass**
- **low driven pass**
- **lofted pass**
- **swerved pass**
- **chipped pass.**

The push pass

The most commonly used pass in the game and the one that is likely to be most accurate. This is mainly because the pass is made with the largest surface of the foot. A very popular pass when used over short distances.

DRILL 1: HIT THE TARGET

Purpose

To improve your technique for using a 'push pass', emphasizing pace and accuracy.

You will need:

4 cones

4 footballs

2 players

Activity

1   Use the cones to make a target area three metres square.

2   Players take turns to pass into the target area, approximately 15 metres away.

3   Each player has two balls and uses the push pass technique.

4   A point is awarded for each ball finishing within the target area.

Think about:

- Approaching the ball at a slight angle.

- Placing your non-kicking foot alongside the ball.

- Keeping your kicking foot turned outwards, showing the inside of the foot.

- Keeping your body over the ball and your eyes focused on the ball.

- Making sure the ankle of the kicking foot remains firm.
- Striking the middle of the ball with the inside of the foot.
- Making sure the kicking foot follows through towards the target area.

Target

How many attempts do you need to score ten points?

Progression

- Reduce the target to a smaller area.
- Try the practice using your weaker foot.
- Try the practice with your team-mate serving a rolling ball to you. Redirect it using 'one touch', towards the target area.

Figure 8.1 **Drill 1: Hit the target**

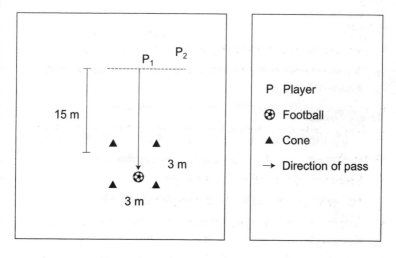

DRILL 2: PASS WITH SPEED

Purpose

To develop your ability to pass the ball at speed using the 'push pass' technique.

You will need:

4 cones

1 football

2 players

Activity

1 Players stand opposite each other, five metres apart just behind the line of the cones.

2 Pass the ball to each other using the 'push pass'.

3 The ball must be kept on the ground and struck firmly to cross the cone line.

4 Carry out the practice for 60 seconds and see how many passes you can make.

5 A point is scored for each pass that crosses the line on the ground.

Think about:

- Using the correct technique as described in 'hitting the target'.
- Not allowing the focus on speed to affect the quality of the pass.
- Remaining on your toes so you can react quickly.
- Making passes firm and accurate.
- Keeping your body and head over the ball.

Target

Can you make 30 passes in a minute?

Progression

- Increase the distance between the cones to ten metres apart.
- Restrict the practice to one-touch/first-time passing – and only count the passes which are completed this way.
- Try the practice using your weaker foot.

Figure 8.2 **Drill 2: Pass with speed**

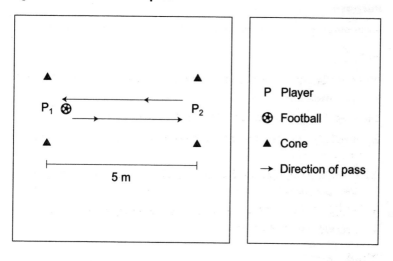

The low driven pass

This type of pass is most useful if a player wants to pass the ball over a longer distance and wants the ball to arrive quickly. The ball stays low to the ground so obviously there needs to be a clear route between the passer and the receiver.

DRILL 3: KNOCK THEM OVER

Purpose

To improve your technique for using the low driven pass, with an emphasis on accuracy.

You will need:

8 cones/boxes/targets

1 football

2 players

Activity

1 Two players stand approximately 15 metres apart, one player with the ball.

2 Targets (cones/boxes) are placed down a line halfway between the players.

3 Targets can be grouped together or left as single targets (harder).

4 Try to knock down each target using the low driven pass technique.

5 Take alternative passes at the targets.

Think about:

- Approaching the ball at a slight angle.
- Keeping your body position over the ball – eyes on the ball.
- Placing your non-kicking foot alongside the ball, though slightly in front.

- Keeping your kicking foot extended, making the pass with the top of your foot.

- Following through with your kicking foot, in the line of the intended target.

- The accuracy of your pass, not just the power.

Target

Can you knock down all eight targets in less than 30 passes?

Progression

- Spread out the targets so they are not grouped together.

- Increase the grid size to 25 metres so you are further away from the targets.

Figure 8.3 **Drill 3: Knock them over**

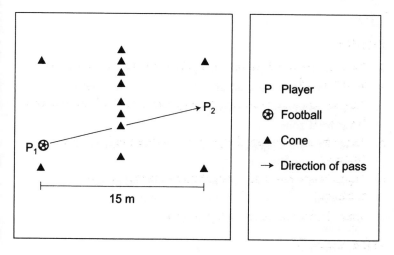

The lofted pass

The lofted pass is most appropriate when players are looking to play a long pass over the head of a player or players, often used when switching play or counter attacking. Many of the top players are able to play extremely accurate passes over long distances into the path of their team-mates.

DRILL 4: LONG BUT ACCURATE

Purpose

To practise the mechanics and technique of the lofted pass with an emphasis on accuracy.

You will need:

4 cones

2 players

6 footballs

Activity

1   Use cones to make a target zone measuring ten metres square.

2   You need to stand 30 metres away and play a lofted pass into the target zone.

3   Player 2 stands behind the target zone and checks that the pass bounces into the zone, acting as a referee.

4   Win a point for every successful long lofted pass. Points are not scored if the ball bounces before reaching the target zone.

Think about:

- Approaching the ball at an angle.
- Keeping your head still and eyes on the ball.
- Taking a larger last stride into the ball to assist with the swinging motion of your kicking leg.

- Placing your non-kicking foot alongside the ball, though slightly behind.

- Making contact with the back of the ball with your instep (top of the foot).

- Remembering to follow through your kicking foot in the line of target.

Target

Keep your score after ten passes and then try to beat your score with a further ten passes.

Progression

- Increase the distance to the target zone.

- Reduce the size of the target zone to five metres square.

Figure 8.4 **Drill 4: Long but accurate**

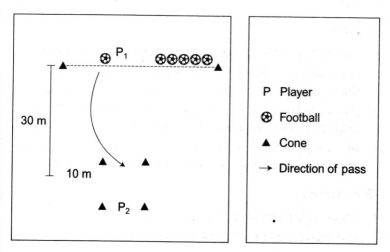

The chipped pass

If players can master the chip pass it has a real advantage over some other passes. The chip pass allows you to play the ball over the opposition's head within a relatively short distance. This pass is extremely difficult to intercept and is ideal for attackers to receive in the last third of the pitch to run on to, beyond the last line of defence.

DRILL 5: CHIP AWAY

Purpose

To practise your technique and accuracy of chipping the ball.

You will need:

4 cones

1 football

2 players

Activity

1　Stand opposite a team-mate in a grid ten metres apart.

2　With a ball at your feet try to chip the ball into the hands of the other player.

3　Player 2 moves along the line between the two cones to present a different target.

4　Score two points each time the ball is caught by the other player.

Think about:

- Approaching the ball at a slight angle.
- Planting your non-kicking foot alongside but slightly in front of the ball.
- Having your head and upper body slightly over the ball.
- The kicking leg being withdrawn more from the knee than the hip.

- The kicking foot making contact with the underside of the ball, via a stabbing action.

- Increasing the backspin on the ball by applying a more powerful stabbing action.

Target

Can you make five consecutive successful chips?

Set yourself a new target, increasing your best score.

Progression

- Your team-mate rolls the ball underarm to you so that the chip pass is made from a moving ball rather than a stationary one.

- Extend the distance to 20 metres.

- Try the practice using your weaker foot.

Figure 8.5 **Drill 5: Chip away**

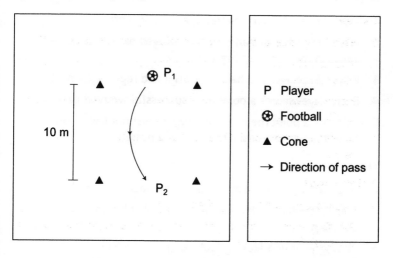

The swerved pass

The swerved pass is another pass that is used over longer distances, with, as its name suggests, a swerve in its flight. This technique is applied when a player wants to swerve the ball around a player or a wall, as the swerved pass is technically the same as a swerved shot.

DRILL 6: CURVE AND SWERVE

Purpose

To practise the required technique to produce a swerved pass.

You will need:

6 cones

1 football

2 players

Activity

1　Two players stand 15 metres apart within a grid.

2　Player 1 has the ball and plays a swerved pass around the two cones in the centre of the grid.

3　Player 2 receives the ball, controls it and repeats the practice.

4　Each player scores a point for a successful swerved pass.

5　To score a point the receiving player must not have to move more than a metre from their starting position.

Think about:

- Approaching the ball at a slight angle, focussing on the ball.
- Making contact with the side of the ball rather than directly behind it.
- Placing your non-kicking foot alongside the ball.
- Contact with the kicking foot is made with the inside or outside of the foot depending which way you are swerving the pass.

Target

Try to make five consecutive point-scoring passes.

Progression

- Widen the distance between the two cones in the centre of the grid, so you will require more swerve on the pass.
- Increase the distance between the two players to 20 metres.
- Try the swerve pass with the outside of the foot.

Figure 8.6 **Drill 6: Curve and swerve**

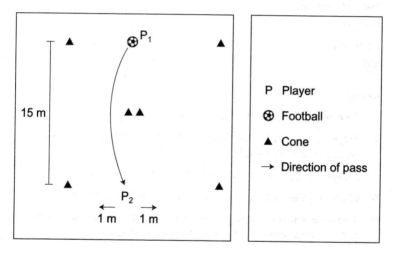

Ball Control

The first touch a player has on the ball is crucial, as it can mean the difference between keeping possession and losing it. If you work on these drills then your technique should improve and you can move to the next stage of deciding what to do with the ball, rather than worrying about your control technique.

The following drills provide you with technique and skills practice to develop your:

- cushion control
- wedge control.

Cushion control

With this method of control a player withdraws or pulls back the surface controlling the ball on impact. This cushions the ball so it falls to the ground in a position where a player can then make their pass, shot or dribble with their next touch. The controlling surface could be the head, chest, thigh or feet.

DRILL 7: CUSHION IT

Purpose

To practise and improve your ability to control the ball using cushion control.

You will need:

4 cones   1 football   2 players

Activity

1. Work with another player inside a ten-metre square grid.
2. The server has the ball and throws it to you underarm, yet above head height, so that you can control it with your thigh.
3. Use cushion control to bring the ball down and pass the ball back to the server.
4. Continue this, moving around the grid.
5. One point is awarded for each successful control.

Think about:

- Getting into the line of the flight of the ball.
- Selecting the controlling surface – your thigh.

- Keeping your eye on the ball as it approaches.
- Being relaxed.
- Withdrawing the thigh as the ball makes contact, to absorb the pace and cushion the ball.
- Making an accurate push pass back to the server.

Target

Ten successful consecutive control and pass manoeuvres.

Progression

- Increase the distance between the two players.
- The server moves around the grid so that you need to look up after controlling the ball to find the server.
- Control using both left and right foot.
- Consider the same activity with different forms of serving, so that different parts of the body are used to practise the cushion control (e.g. chest or inside foot).

Figure 8.7 **Drill 7: Cushion it**

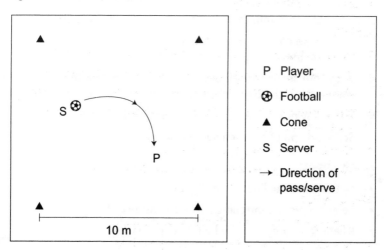

P Player

⊛ Football

▲ Cone

S Server

→ Direction of pass/serve

10 m

Wedge control

Another method of controlling the ball, when time and space is available, is the wedge control. A player pushes out the surface chosen (head, chest, thigh or foot) to control the ball, so that the ball is redirected into the space for the player's second touch.

DRILL 8: WEDGE WORKS

Purpose

To develop your ability to bring the ball under control using the wedge technique.

You will need:

4 cones

1 football

2 players

Activity

1　Stand approximately 20 metres away from a team-mate.

2　Move towards your team-mate and receive a pass to your feet.

3　Use wedge control, redirecting the ball out of your feet with your first touch.

4　With your second touch pass the ball back to your team-mate who controls the ball before passing it back to you.

5　Keep moving back to your line to receive the pass.

6　Score one point for each successful control.

Think about:

- Getting into the line of the flight of the ball.
- Selecting your controlling surface – inside of foot.
- Keeping your eye on the ball as it approaches.

- Tensing the controlling surface – the foot – as you receive the ball.
- Redirecting the ball out in front of you.

Target

Be confident receiving the ball on your weaker side.

Keep a score out of ten passes. Can you beat that score for another set of ten passes?

Progression

- Increase the speed of the practice.
- Use your right and left foot alternately.
- Increase the size of the grid and move freely around the area – varying the serve to the thigh, chest and feet.

Figure 8.8 **Drill 8: Wedge works**

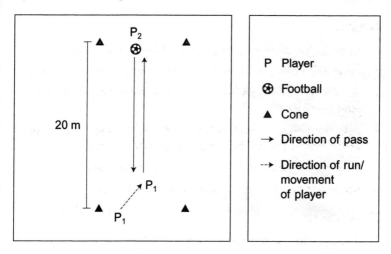

Heading

Statistic

Over 20 per cent of all goals scored are headers.

People will often comment that football is at its best when the ball is played on the floor. However, there are inevitably going to be situations in a game when the ball is played in the air through goal kicks, free kicks, corners, long throws, crosses and clearances.

Heading the ball is generally divided into two categories – defensive heading and attacking heading, though there are some common principles which apply to both. If the correct technique is followed, then heading a football will not hurt and with regular practice, a player's confidence will grow.

Whether you are making a defensive or attacking header it is important that you follow the basic technique:

- Be prepared to attack the ball.
- The movement of the neck muscles provide the power, supported by some upper body movement/arched back.
- The ball should come into the contact with the forehead because this is the largest and flattest part of the head surface, enabling the player to control their heading and provide accuracy.
- After contact is made with the ball, there should be a follow-through of the head along the line of the intended target.

A defensive header

DRILL 9: BASIC HEADING

Purpose

To develop confidence and practise the basic heading technique.

You will need:

4 cones

1 football

2 players

Activity

1 Players stand opposite each other within a five-metre square grid.

2 Player 1 throws the ball underarm to player 2 who heads the ball back.

3 Players alternate roles with player 2 throwing the ball to player 1.

4 Players score a point for every successful header.

Think about:

* Watching the ball.

* Moving into the line of the ball.

* Keeping your eyes open.

* Heading the ball with the forehead.

* Aiming to make contact with the middle of the ball.

* Attacking the ball with purpose.

Target

Ten consecutive, accurate headers to your partner.

Progression

Increase the distance between the two players to ten metres.

Figure 8.9 **Drill 9: Basic heading**

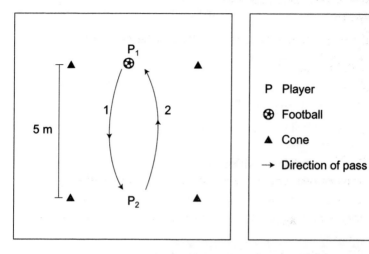

The following drills will encourage you to develop confidence and good technique when heading the football, whether you are in a defensive or attacking situation.

Defensive headers

As a defending player, particularly when the ball is close to your team's penalty area, it is important to:

- head the ball high, which allows time for defending team-mates to reorganize
- head the ball long, which takes the ball further away from the danger area
- head the ball wide, either out of play or to a safe angle from the goal.

DRILL 10: HEADING FOR SAFETY

Purpose

To improve the technique involved when heading for distance.

You will need:

4 cones

1 football

3 players

Activity

1 Player 2 serves the ball for player 1 to head.

2 Player 1 tries to head the ball beyond the server to player 3.

3 Player 3 collects the ball and returns it to player 2 to continue the practice.

4 Rotate positions every ten headers.

5 Players score a point for clearing the middle player and two points for reaching player 3.

Think about:

- Heading the ball high.
- Heading the ball long.
- Attacking the ball with confidence.
- Running to meet the ball.
- Slightly arching your back and tightening your neck muscles.
- Accurate serving.

Target

The first player to reach ten points after an equal number of turns.

Progression

Continue using three players, but slightly reorganize the roles. Player 2 stands just in front of player 1 but remains static. Player 3 becomes the server. As player 3 serves the ball to Player 1, Player 1 jumps to head clear. Players rotate roles. The role of Player 2 can change so they can offer more resistance by also jumping to distract Player 1.

Figure 8.10 **Drill 10: Heading for safety**

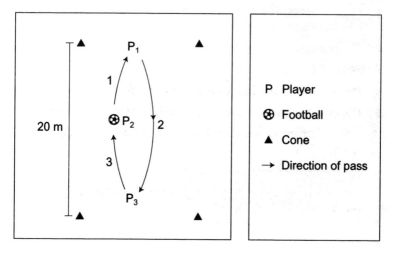

Flick-on headers

The flick-on header is used in a variety of different situations. Players may use the technique in an attacking situation, to head towards goal from either a corner or long throw. Alternatively, a forward may use the flick-on header to put a team-mate through on goal, flicking the ball beyond the last defender.

In defensive situations, a player may use the flick-on header to head the ball backwards to their goalkeeper as a safe way of keeping possession.

DRILL 11: FLICK IT ON

Purpose

To improve the technique involved in flick-on headers.

You will need:

4 cones

1 football

3 players

Activity

1   Player 1 serves the ball underarm to player 2 who stands in the middle of a ten-metre square grid.

2   Player 2 heads the ball to player 3 with a flick-on header.

3   Player 3 collects the ball and serves it to player 2.

4   Players rotate their positions after ten headers.

5   One point is scored for accurate flick-on headers reaching the intended targets.

Think about:

*   Moving quickly into the flight of the ball.
*   Using one foot to take off as you jump.
*   Trying to head the ball at its highest point.
*   Using your forehead to deflect the ball.

- Tilting your head back so the ball glances off your forehead towards the intended target.

Target

First player to reach ten points after an equal number of turns.

Progression

Introduce a defender by moving player 3 to stand behind player 2. Player 2 then tries to flick the ball on and over player 3, making it a more realistic game situation.

Figure 8.11 **Drill 11: Flick it on**

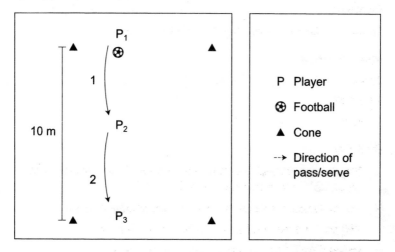

Attacking headers

When teams are attacking in the last third of the pitch, they will often find that space on the ground is harder to find. As a deliberate tactic they will look to put the ball in the air, particularly in and around the penalty area.

Players who head the ball in attacking situations are usually looking for accuracy, either on goal or into the path of another player on their team. Headers on goal which are aimed downwards are generally the most difficult to save.

DRILL 12: HEADING AT A TARGET

Purpose

To develop heading technique with emphasis on accuracy.

You will need:

10 cones or boxes

1 football

2 players

Activity

1 Players stand facing each other inside a ten-metre square grid apart.

2 Player 1 throws the ball up for headers at a target area in the centre of the grid.

3 Player 2 collects the ball and repeats the practice.

4 Two points are scored for every successful header. The ball must not bounce before reaching the target area.

5 Develop the practice with players serving to each other and heading towards the target.

Think about:

- Establishing a well-balanced stance.
- Releasing the ball out of your hands.

- Attacking the ball with your forehead and with your eyes open.
- Developing the power by swinging your upper body backwards and then forwards.
- Developing your jump so that you get your timing right.

Target

First player to score ten points.

Progression

Use four cones to mark out two three-metre wide goals, ten metres apart. Players cannot use their hands when defending their goal. Player 1 serves the ball from the goal-line to player 2, who heads the ball down and past player 1, towards the corner of the goal.

Two points are given for every goal scored, one point for every saved header on target.

First player to get ten points after an equal number of turns.

Figure 8.12 **Drill 12: Heading at a target**

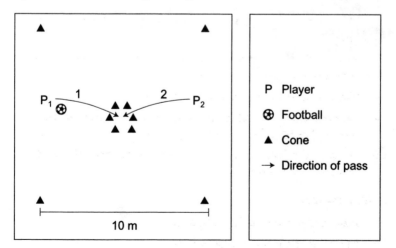

Diving headers

All heading is about attacking the ball, and possibly the best example of this is the diving header, where the whole body is committed to the ball. The diving header is often seen as an attacking skill, though it can be used in defensive situations to prevent goals being scored.

DRILL 13: DIVING PAYS

Purpose

To develop the technique and confidence to produce a diving header.

You will need:

4 cones

1 football

2 players

Activity

1 Players face each other ten metres apart.

2 Player 1 throws the ball to player 2. The ball should drop just in front of player 2.

3 Player 2 attempts to score past player 1 with a diving header.

4 Two points are given for every goal scored, one point for every header on target.

Think about:

- Making the serves accurate.
- Keeping your eye on the ball.
- Trying to head the top of the ball, forcing it downwards.
- Heading the ball with your forehead with eyes open.
- Dropping your arms to cushion your fall.
- Aiming for the corner of the goal.
- Attacking the header in a committed way.

Target

Reaching ten points after ten attempts.

Progression

Introduce two more players, widen the goals and play 2 v 2 – taking it in turns to serve to each other in your teams to score diving headers.

Figure 8.13 **Drill 13: Diving pays**

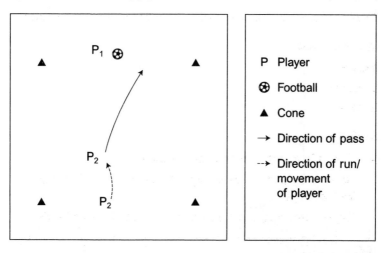

Defending

Regardless of the position you play in your team, it is important that you accept the responsibility of defending whenever your team is not in possession. It is not only defenders and midfield players who are required to defend, demands on forward players to close down opponents and make tackles is also part of the modern game. Chapter 7 looked at the individual techniques associated with tackling – timing, block tackle and slide tackle. The following drills should help you try to develop good practice associated with defending in 1 v 1 situations.

| Quote | Tips for a full-back in a 1 v 1 situation in a wide area of the pitch *'Do not lose the race, be patient, you do not necessarily need to tackle. Delay and block is acceptable defending as this gives your team time to regroup. Do not gamble on a challenge.'* Martin Allen |

Defending 1 v 1 situations

Having the individual skills to defend 1 v 1 situations is a real strength that a player brings to his or her team. Here are some of the most important principles:

- **Gain as much ground as possible on your opponent while the ball is travelling.**
- **Slow down as you approach the player, approximately two metres away.**
- **Get low by bending your knees.**
- **Adopt a side-on body position which will prevent the attacker from turning or getting ahead of you.**
- **Try to make the direction of the play predictable and force the player wide, away from your goal.**
- **Consider when the time is right to make the tackle.**
- **Remain positive and aggressive about your desire to win the tackle.**

DRILL 14: HOLD THEM UP

Purpose

To develop your ability to defend 1 v 1 situations.

You will need:

6 cones

1 football

2 players

Activity

1 Use four cones to make a ten-metre square grid and two cones to make a target three metres wide.

2 The server stands on one side of the grid and passes the ball to player 1 standing on the end line opposite the goal.

3 As soon as the pass is made the server runs to the centre of the grid and becomes a defender.

4 Player 1 uses turns to try to dribble round the defender.

5 The defender scores one point every time they win possession and player 1 scores one point when they dribble the ball through the target.

Think about:

- Good defending principles – referred to above – defending 1 v 1 situations.
- Moving in quickly to pressurize the attacker.
- 'Jockeying' for position.
- Being patient and not diving in.
- Challenging when you get the right opportunity.
- Being positive about winning the tackle.

Target

First player to reach five points, then alternate roles.

Progression

- Vary the position of the server so the defender experiences 1 v 1 situations – side by side, face to face, and behind the attacker's back.

- Move the target goal to the centre of the grid and make the goal a one-metre square grid. The defender has to prevent the attacker from dribbling through any side of the target goal.

Figure 8.14 **Drill 14: Hold them up**

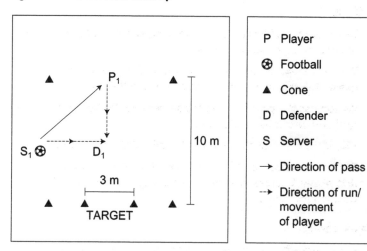

Tracking back

Players all over the pitch are required to track back. This quite simply means that when your team has lost possession of the ball and, particularly if the opposition is looking to counter attack, then all players should be prepared to get back behind the ball as quickly as possible. Tracking back denies the opposition the opportunity to mount effective counter attacks.

The skills required include:

- turning skills
- speed
- stamina
- tackling ability
- determination.

DRILL 15: TRACK BACK

Purpose

To develop your ability to chase back quickly after losing possession.

You will need:

4 cones

1 football

2 players

Activity

1　Players stand either end of a 20-metre × 5-metre grid.

2　Player 2 has the ball and dribbles it to approximately five metres away from player 1.

3　Player 2 passes the ball to player 1 and then stands with legs apart.

4　Player 1 receives the pass and kicks it through the legs of player 2.

5　Player 1 sprints to retrieve the ball and continues towards the opposite end of the grid.

6　Player 2 turns and tracks back, sprinting after player 1, trying to reach the end line of the grid before player 1.

7　The practice is physically intensive so have rest periods between each run. Alternate players' roles.

Think about:

- Turning quickly.
- Accelerating with good running style.
- Being determined to get back, ahead of the attacker.
- Never giving in, as the attacker may lose control of the ball.
- Forcing the direction of the attacker's run.

Target

Win at least 50 per cent of the races.

Progression

Introduce tackling into the practice. The chasing player will have to consider where and when to tackle.

Figure 8.15 **Drill 15: Track back**

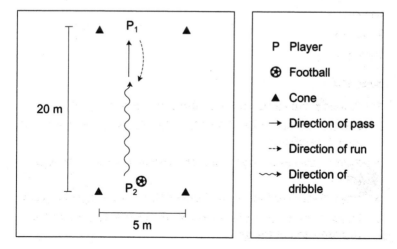

Jockeying the attacker

In Chapter 7, the football fundamental of tackling is considered, providing technical details on tackling. One of the areas it refers to is timing of the tackle and 'jockeying' attackers.

A defender's first task is to delay the attacker, keeping their body between the attacker and the goal, backing off slightly as the attacker moves forward. This delaying tactic allows team-mates to get back to support the defender by getting other players back behind the ball. Drill 14: Hold them up helps you to practise this vital defensive skill.

Shielding the ball

Players who have the technical ability and strength to shield the ball so that supporting players can come and support them are vital to their team, particularly when trying to keep possession. Having the ability to shield the ball is a combination of a good first touch, accompanied by body strength to fend off other players.

Try the following drill with your team-mate to develop your technique for shielding the ball.

DRILL 16: HOLD THEM OFF AND LOOK FOR SUPPORT

Purpose:

To develop your ability to shield the ball until support arrives.

You will need:

4 cones

3 players

1 football

Activity

1   Players 1 and 2 stand one metre apart in the centre of a ten-metre square grid. The server stands on the side of the grid.

2   The server plays the ball to the feet of player 1.

3   Player 2 closes player 1 down by moving in quickly.

4   Player 1 tries to shield the ball, holding off player 2.

5   After 20 seconds player 1 can play the ball back to the server and collect a point.

6   Player 2 gets a point if they win the ball inside the 20 seconds.

7   Alternate players' roles.

Think about:

- Making sure you are the first to the ball.

- Leaning back slightly and bending your knees.

- Using your arms and body as a barrier to fend off the defender.

- Concentrating on a good first touch so the ball remains in close control.

- Keeping your body between the ball and the defender.

Target

First player to reach five points after equal turns.

Progression

- Create a goal or target on the opposite side of the grid to the server.

- The server plays the ball to player 1 who shields the ball from player 2, the defender.

- After 20 seconds of shielding, player 1 passes the ball back to the server who then takes a strike on goal.

Figure 8.16 **Drill 15: Hold them off and look for support**

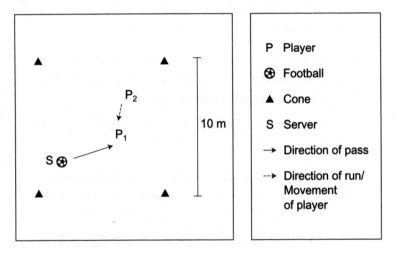

Summary

This chapter has looked at a variety of different skills required, some fundamental to all positions, others more specific to defending. Here are some tips and reminders for these skills.

Passing

- When passing to your team-mate, try to pass to their foot which is furthest away from your opponent.

- When passing to a player in space, try to pass to the space just in front of them so they can collect the pass as they run, without having to break their stride.

- The safest and most accurate way of passing is to use the inside of the foot.

- When linking up with team-mates, try to use the whole pitch, switching play and using the width, as this makes it difficult for the opposition to get close to the ball.

- Fast and safe passes will generally out-play the opposition.

- Remember, as soon as you have played a pass, get ready to take up a new position to receive another – pass and move.

Receiving the ball

- Always try to receive the ball with an open body position, unless you are tightly marked.

- Move to meet the ball rather than wait for it.

- Try to use cushion control in tight situations when you do not want the ball to go far away from you.

- Use wedge control when the space is available to you, pushing the ball away from your opponent and into the space.

- Always have your toe slightly raised on your receiving foot, so that the ball doesn't bounce over your foot.

- Be prepared to use different surfaces to control the ball by getting into the line of the ball early.

- Try not to lose time by letting high balls bounce; get them down under control and use the time to your advantage.

Heading

- Defensive headers, close to your penalty area should be headed high, long and wide.

- Attacking headers are about accuracy, so try to head them down for a team-mate or, if heading at the goal, down towards the ground to make it more difficult for a goalkeeper to save.

- Always attack the header, using the forehead and keeping the eyes open.

Defending 1 v 1

- Don't just charge towards your opponent thinking they will lose possession. Wait for a good chance for you to win the ball.

- Try to make up ground on your opponent as the ball is travelling towards them – you may intercept it or you may tackle the player if they lose control of it. It pays to wait.

- **Be prepared to drop back if an opponent is dribbling towards you. Use a jockeying technique to delay them. Don't get square on to them.**

- **Only go to ground if it is the last option. Always try to stay on your feet when making the challenge.**

- **Try to force your opponent away from the goal so they can't get in to a position to shoot.**

- **Watch the ball rather than the player's movements.**

Self-tester

- What is the difference between wedge control and cushion control?
- What is the purpose of 'jockeying' an attacker?
- What are the main aims of a defensive header?

Action plan

Plan a seven-week training programme for yourself based around the seven areas highlighted in this chapter:

- passing
- ball control
- heading
- defending
- tracking back
- jockeying the attacker
- shielding the ball.

Focus on each area for a week, reading the tips on techniques and choosing some of the drills to practise the skills.

Chapter 9

Tactics and teamwork

THIS CHAPTER WILL:
- Highlight some tactics and support play that will help you to become an effective defender within a team.
- Provide drills and practices for you and your team-mates to try to support the above.
- Consider the decisions that defenders need to make during a match, both in possession and out of possession.

Forcing the play

If a team is going to make play predictable they must work together and communicate between each other. The individual roles for each player will change depending where the ball is, and who the nearest player is.

The basic principles of defending are:

- **pressure** – pressurizing the player on the ball (first defender)
- **support** – supporting the pressurizing player (second defender)
- **cover** – covering in the space behind the supporting player (third defender).

Figure 9.1 **The position of three defenders making play predictable**

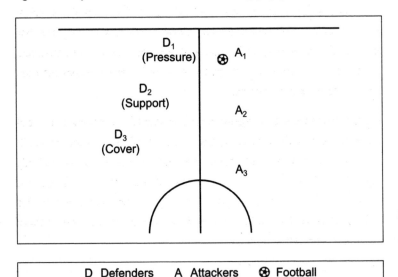

Forcing the play is generally the responsibility of the first defender who pressurizes the player on the ball. It is their decision and actions that will directly affect how successful a team is in forcing the play. For example, a first defender who does not pressurize quickly, will allow their opponent the time to explore the space and possibly move into the dangerous areas of the pitch. If a defender pressurizes early, making progress as the ball travels to their opponent, they may be able to stop a player turning. If this happens, then the first defender has successfully forced the play. In stopping the ball being played forward, you then allow your team-mates to get back behind the ball and offer the support and cover required for good defending.

There are times when a defender's body position and angle of approach will dictate where the ball is played next. It will not always be possible for you, as the first defender, to prevent the ball from being played forward, and you may even encourage a forward pass. For example, a striker working as the first defender may allow a full-back to play the ball forward, down the line, rather than let them switch play across the pitch, as the forward pass into a relatively restricted space is easier for their team-mates to defend against.

The first defender may also prevent an opponent from making a pass, but may not feel that the time is right to make a challenge on the player. In this situation you should attempt to use your angle of approach and body position to force a player into the areas of the pitch considered less dangerous. For example, a full-back putting pressure on a player on the ball would be advised to force them down the line rather than let them cut across them and cut infield.

Top tip

Always remember, you should wait for the right time to make your tackle.

The supporting defender and covering defender should constantly be giving information to the pressurizing player, advising them of their supporting positions and encouraging them to force the play into the less dangerous area, such as out to the wings or, better still, backwards.

Quote | 'With two central defenders balance is needed – one to cover, one to challenge.'
David Moyes

DRILL 1: FORCE THE PLAY

Purpose

To improve a defender's skill in 1 v 1 situations

You will need:

4 cones

1 football

4 players or more

1 goal

Activity

1   The defending group is positioned at one corner where the penalty area meets the touchline. The attacking group is positioned diagonally opposite.

2   D1 passes to A1 and follows their pass.

3   D1 tries to prevent A1 from scoring a goal.

4   You score a point as a defender if you dispossess the attacker.

Key points for defenders

- Gain as much ground as possible as the ball is travelling.

- Keep your body between the ball and the goal and adopt a 'side-on' position.

- Slow down when you get within touching distance of A1.

- Get low with bent knees.

- Make the direction of play for A1 predictable, away from your goal.

- Wait for an appropriate moment to make your tackle.

Progression

- Advance the practice to a 2 v 2 situation.

- Keep the same key points, though stressing the importance of communication.

- The second defender provides support and cover.

Figure 9.2 **Drill 1: Force the play**

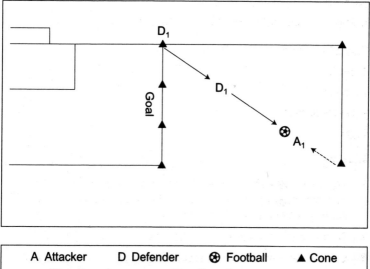

A Attacker	D Defender	⊗ Football	▲ Cone
→ Direction of pass	--→ Direction of run		

Player-to-player marking

There are two defensive methods that a team may choose to use:

- **zonal**
- **man-to-man/player-to-player.**

With both systems the individuals in the team will have specific roles. The ability to read the game and keep up good communication between all players is vital.

> **Quote** | 'Reading the game is essential – be proactive, not reactive. Sometimes defenders with pace are just reactive and rely on their pace to get them out of trouble.'
> Steve McClaren

The zonal system involves all players taking responsibility for an area on the pitch. These are mainly the areas in and around their specific position, with a player marking opponents as they enter their 'zone'. The man-to-man marking method requires each player to take defensive responsibility for one of the opposition players.

Whichever system your team plays, good defending principles are required.

You should always consider:

- **staying goal side**
- **staying close**
- **looking to intercept**
- **applying pressure**
- **looking to tackle when opportunity arises**
- **staying on your feet.**

Man-to-man marking is likely to be the system that gives you the greatest chance of intercepting the ball. Your starting position is relatively close to your opponent, and therefore your chance to intercept the ball will increase. However, if you get too close your opponent may take the opportunity to turn away from you, using their upper body and arms to hold you off. It is therefore important that you do not over commit, or get too close. Your opponent needs to feel that you are close enough to tackle them if they turn or lose control of the ball – this is often called 'touch close'. Try Drill 2 to practise the techniques of player-to-player marking.

DRILL 2: PLAYER-TO-PLAYER MARKING

Purpose

To develop man-to-man marking skills.

You will need:

10 cones

1 football

10 players

set of bibs

Activity

1   Divide players into two teams (A and B) and mark out a pitch 30 metres × 40 metres.

2   Mark out small target goals at each end of the pitch.

3   Every player has one opponent whom they are responsible for marking; they can only tackle that player and vice versa.

4   The practice develops man-to-man marking skills and exposes any player who is not working hard for their team.

Key points for defenders

- Keep goal side.
- Try to anticipate your player's next move.
- Look to intercept.
- Try to prevent your player from turning.
- Pressurize your opponent when they get the ball.

Figure 9.3 **Drill 2: Player-to-player marking**

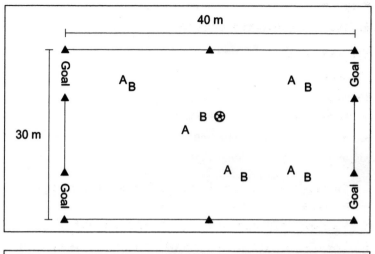

1 v 2 defending

There will be occasions in a game when your opponents will outnumber you. What you choose to do in this situation will have a direct impact on the success and outcome of the attack.

Unless one of your opponents loses control of the ball, you may find it difficult to win possession. However, there are good practices that you can follow to help your team. Ultimately, if you can slow down the attack you will be providing time for your team-mates to get back to support you and create a better defending situation which should ideally see pressure, support and cover in place.

Try this next drill to see how successful you and your team-mates are at holding up the attack.

DRILL 3: HOLD UP THE ATTACK

Purpose

To improve a defender's skill in 1 v 2 situations.

You will need:

6 cones

1 football

6 or more players

Activity

1 A group of defenders are at one end of the grid and a group of attackers at the other.

2 A defender passes the ball to one of the two attackers at the opposite end of the grid.

3 After passing the ball, the defender, D1, tries to prevent the two attackers A1 and A2 from reaching the end line.

4 A second defender is released from the attackers' end to support the lone defender after ten seconds of the practice starting.

5 The defender wins a point after tackling or forcing the attackers to lose possession.

6 D3, D4 and A3, A4 rotate with other players to avoid fatigue.

Key points for defenders

- Gain as much ground as possible after making your pass.
- Slow down when 'touching distance' away from your attacker.
- Adopt a good defensive position, side on, get low with knees bent.
- Try to make play predictable.
- Keep both of the attackers in your view at all times.
- Can you hold up the attack until the second defender assists you?

Progression

Develop the practice of a 2 v 2 defending drill – (see page 174).

Figure 9.4 **Drill 3: Hold up the attack**

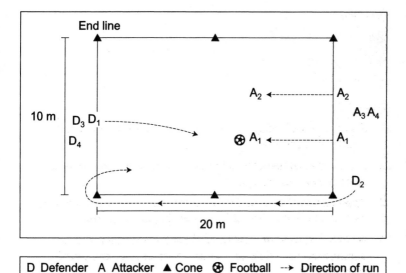

D Defender   A Attacker   ▲ Cone   ✪ Football   --→ Direction of run

2 v 2 defending

Though 2 v 2 situations are not ideal for defending teams, they are an improvement on the 1 v 2 situation referred to above. Once again, there are some fundamental defending principles that you and your team-mates should follow which will lead to effective defending. The principles need to be practised on a regular basis and your coach should be encouraged to work on defending practices and positioning just as much as the more popular attacking and shooting drills.

Earlier in the chapter we referred to the pressure, support and cover roles provided by three players in a defending situation. The 2 v 2 situation, which you are likely to find yourself in on several occasions during a match, requires you to modify these roles for the two defending players. The next drill provides you with a chance to develop your 2 v 2 defensive techniques, providing some kind of pressure, support and cover to cope with the attack.

DRILL 4: PRESSURE, SUPPORT AND COVER

Purpose

To improve defensive positioning in 2 v 2 situations.

You will need:

6 cones   1 football   a minimum of 4 players

Activity

1   Four players work in a 10-metre × 20-metre grid.
2   Two players represent attackers and start at one end; the other two are defenders and start at the opposite end of the grid.
3   The two attackers slowly dribble the ball forward, passing the ball between them.
4   The two defenders slowly retreat, with the emphasis on keeping correct defensive positions. There is no tackling.

Key points for defenders

- Players need to adjust their defensive position quickly as the ball is passed between the attackers. You should do this as the ball is travelling.
- The supporting defender needs to communicate to the pressurizing defender.
- Adopt a good defensive stance – pivot on your back foot when changing direction.
- The nearest defender to the ball is the pressurizing defender.
- The supporting (covering) defender should always be in a position to cover the pressurizing defender and also mark their own attacker.

Figure 9.5 **Drill 4: Pressure, support and cover**

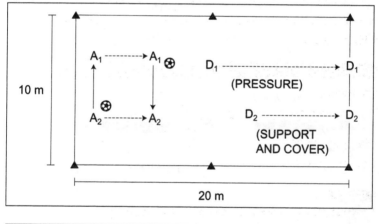

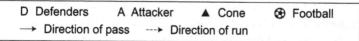

Progression

- Increase the speed of the practice.
- Make the practice competitive and introduce tackling.

The defensive shape and balance of a back four

The team formations and systems used by most teams have been highlighted on pages 12–24. Each of the systems, whether three, four or five players are in defence, provides some form of balance and positional team shape to deal with different attacking situations.

The following drills will help your team develop their defensive shape and balance, and can be modified to suit different formations. The drills provide you and your coach with the opportunity to put into practice some of the defending principles we have already looked at. These drills are introduced in a relatively confined area (penalty area) and also in an 11 v 11 situation, when four defenders are confronted with an attack involving four players across the full width of the pitch.

With these defending situations, players should realize that the pattern of play is forever changing and that their individual movement and roles change with every pass made. Concentration and team communication are extremely important.

DRILL 5: KEEP THE SHAPE (CONFINED AREA)

Purpose

To improve defender's positioning and challenging around penalty area.

You will need:

several footballs   12 players

Activity

1   The practice takes place within a penalty area, involving eight outfield players, a goalkeeper and three servers.

2   S1, S2 and S3 take it in turns to serve the ball to any of the attackers. When the ball has been played the four defenders react accordingly, depending on the position of the ball.

3 Attackers try to score, with a point given for every goal scored. A point is given to defenders for regaining possession.

Key points for defenders

- Closest defender pressurizes the ball.
- Closest defender delays the attack.
- Other defenders offer support and cover the first defender.
- Marking should be goal-side and within touching distance.
- Defenders look to intercept whenever they can.
- Servers should vary the pass they make into the attack.

Progression

Similar practice 4 v 4 but played on the full width of the pitch.

Figure 9.6 **Drill 5: Keep the shape (confined area)**

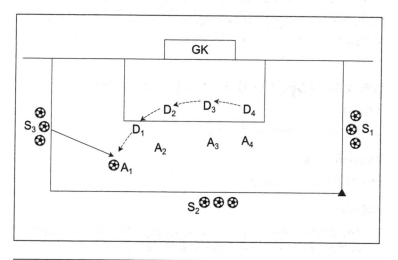

A Attacker   D Defender   S Server   ▲ Cone   ⊗ Football
GK Goalkeeper   --▶ Direction of run   → Direction of pass

DRILL 6: KEEP THE SHAPE (FULL WIDTH)

Purpose

To improve the defensive shape of the back four defenders.

You will need:

half of the pitch

a minimum of 12 outfield players

goalkeeper

several footballs

Activity

1 A line is marked with cones dividing the playing area in half.

2 Four defenders are in the defending half with four attackers at the end line. The four attackers move towards the defenders with the ball, attacking the goal.

3 Their objective is to score a goal. If they score they remain as attackers, but if they do not score and lose possession they change roles with the defenders who then join the attacking group.

4 Attackers A5, A6, A7 and A8 keep rotating with other players every five minutes.

Key points for defenders

- The back four should be spread evenly across the pitch.
- Depending on the position of the ball, the closest defender should pressurize the player on the ball. The 'second' defender should add support, with the other defenders providing cover and balance to the defensive unit.
- Decisions need to be made about when to challenge.
- Communication is needed from players behind the pressurizing defender, advising them where to face the attacker, inside, down the line etc.
- The position of back four players should change in relation to the position of the ball.

Figure 9.7 **Drill 6: Keep the shape (full width)**

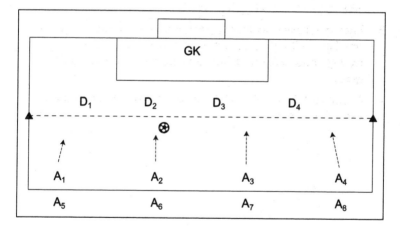

A Attacker	D Defender	S Server	⊛ Football
GK Goalkeeper	--→ Direction of run	→ Direction of pass	

Figures 9.8 and 9.9 show the desired position of the back four when the ball is in a wide position and when it is in a central position.

Figure 9.8 **The defensive shape of the back four when the ball is in a wide position**

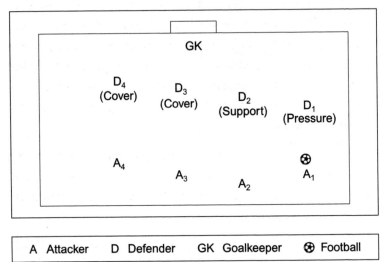

A Attacker   D Defender   GK Goalkeeper   ⊕ Football

Figure 9.9 **The defensive shape of the back four when the ball is in a central position**

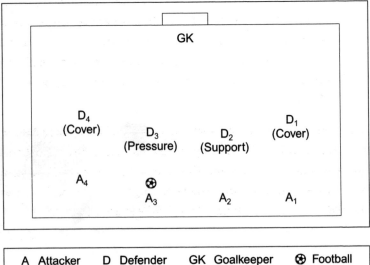

A Attacker   D Defender   GK Goalkeeper   ⊕ Football

Defending as a team

Closing down and defending as a team is essential if your team wants to win back possession from the opposition. To be effective, closing down needs to be methodical, involving the whole team, with players prepared to work hard in all positions. Any part of the game that requires teamwork and tactics needs to be practised so that the team is organized, with each player knowing their role and having an understanding between each other.

Defending and regaining possession can be physically quite demanding and one thing that players soon realize is how important it is not to give possession away easily. The better your team is at keeping possession, the less defending your team will have to do.

A team can choose one of two options as a defensive tactic, high pressure and low pressure.

High pressure

If teams choose to play with high pressure, your coach will be encouraging you and your team-mates to try to win the ball back as close to the opposition's goal as possible. This involves all the players in your team and requires them to have a high work rate. You need to reduce the time and space your opponents have on the ball and make the play as predictable as possible. Denying the opposition space is a principle of good defensive play.

If a defending team manages to win the ball back high up the pitch, an advantage they have is that they can quickly attack their opposition's goal after regaining possession. This tactic is likely to be used by a team that is losing with only a few minutes of the game remaining, but it can be used at any time by a team with fit, hard-working players.

Low pressure

A defence that has players that drop back and retreat after losing possession is operating a low-pressure form of defending. With this system, whoever is closest to the attacking player when possession is lost will try to delay the opposition's attack. This will allow other players in the defending team to get behind the ball and reform the defence. The space the players are defending is likely to be a reduced one compared with the space in a high-pressure system. The retreating players should be aiming to defend with a compact team shape.

As soon as the ball is lost, all players look to retreat and get back behind the ball. The first defender 'jockeys' the opponent to create time for other players to get back into their defensive positions. Whenever the defending team regains possession the retreating stops and, at this point, it is common for a defending team to launch some kind of counter attack. With the space available in front of them this can be very effective.

Top tip

As with all good defending teams, whatever tactic or style you are adopting, you need to be well organized and communicate with each other throughout a match.

The following practice will allow your team to try out both high-pressure and low-pressure defending. It also rewards teams that prevent their opponents from having attempts on goal.

DRILL 7: STOP THE SHOT

Purpose

To practise defensive skills and prevent shots on goal.

You will need:

2 goals

14 players including 2 goalkeepers

bibs

cones

1 football

Activity

1   Create a playing area approximately 20-metres square with a goal at either end, both with a goalkeeper.

2   Four attackers play against four defenders, and two additional defenders stand either side of the goal at both ends.

3   The defending team passes the ball to the attacking team and the practice starts.

4   The attacking team is trying to score, while the defending team is trying to prevent shots on goal.

5   After the attacking team has taken five passes, the two extra defenders (D5 + D6) come onto the pitch to create a 6 v 4 situation in favour of defenders.

6   After 2 goes, rotate so that attackers become defenders and defenders become attackers.

Key points for defenders

•   Try closing the ball down after the initial pass is made.

•   The closest defender pressurizes and delays the attack.

•   Other defenders offer support and cover.

- Good communication needed among the defenders.
- Keep the defensive shape – this will change as the ball position changes.
- Stay compact, don't let the attackers come through you.
- Try to force the attackers away from goal.
- Stay on your feet and wait for the right time to challenge.

Progression

- Introduce more players to the practice to make it 6 v 6.
- Make the playing area larger.
- Two-touch condition – defending team readjusts their position quicker.

Figure 9.10 **Drill 7: Stop the shot**

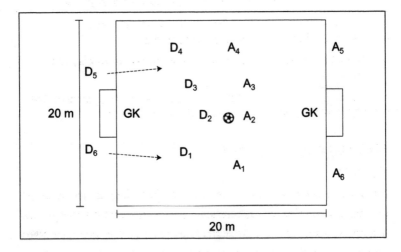

| A | Attacker | D | Defender | GK | Goalkeeper | ⊕ Football |

Playing as a sweeper

In defensive terms the benefits of using a sweeper can never be understated. With individual and team defending, and with tactics such as playing the offside trap, it is important that there are players in the team who take responsibility for organizing others around them and making team decisions.

Some teams play with a sweeper who drops back beyond a central defender, whereas other systems may see them playing behind two central defenders. Either way, there are certain characteristics that a good sweeper has that benefits the whole team:

- The 'extra' player who covers mistakes made in front of them.
- The player who provides consistent defensive cover, giving confidence to the other players to go forward and attack.
- The player who will often be heard passing important information to team-mates all around them.
- The player who can decide when and when not to play the offside trap.
- The player who has the technical ability and composure on the ball to bring it out of defence and start an attack.

Defending set plays

Corners

Like many set-play situations, the secret to defending corners is to get organized as quickly as possible and concentrate until the danger has passed. All teams can practise defending corners, and a well-drilled and well-organized team can have success defending what can be a dangerous set play.

There are two choices that a team can make when it is defending corners – **player-to-player** and **zonal** – both of which have been referred to earlier in this chapter. Teams should practise both to see which their team prefers. With player-to-player marking at corners, a player stays with the opponent assigned to them, no matter where they go, in and around the penalty area. The zonal option has players defending an allocated space around the penalty area. They attack the ball if it comes into their space, irrespective of how many or how close the attackers are.

As soon as a corner kick is conceded it is vital that your team gets organized quickly. Wasting vital seconds could be the difference between your opposition scoring or not. The goalkeeper has an important role to play when defending corners, not just as someone who may come and collect or punch the ball clear, but also to organize the defenders and gives commands like 'head away' or 'keeper's ball'.

Most of the roles and positions that defending players occupy can be established before a match starts, with well-practised drills. However, a team needs to be able to react quickly to situations that may occur if the opposition is clever and inventive at corner kicks. Some of the most common defensive positions adopted for corner kicks are as follows:

- A player challenges the attacking player taking the corner kick (ten metres away) in an attempt to cut out the cross.
- Two players are placed on each post to assist with protecting the goal.
- Other players either mark a space (zonal) or opt for the man-to-man method.
- Central strikers take a defensive role. You will often see one of the strikers come back to assist with defending the corner. They are often tall and good in the air – an obvious advantage to the defending team.

Throw-ins

Just like corner kicks and any set play situation, the important consideration for a defending team is to 'switch on' and concentrate the second the ball has gone out of play. This immediate organization of your team can prevent dangerous attacks from being built. Most of the issues should be well known to a player, as each role should be discussed in coaching and training sessions. Leaving the roles unclear until match day is not recommended.

If a team is defending long throw-ins, good practice is very similar to defending a corner. A defending team may opt for one player to stand in front of, and another behind, the player that the throw is aimed at. This same practice can be used in other situations around the pitch in an attempt to stop the ball being thrown down the line to a player's feet.

As a defending player at a throw-in you should:

- **be ready to react to the movement of the player closest to you**
- **identify the players that you and your team-mates are marking**
- **be prepared to pass a player on to another defender if their opponent and your opponent switch positions**
- **communicate to your team-mates, including calling for the ball, if you are making a challenge to head the ball clear.**

Free kicks

Getting organized quickly and identifying your individual role is essential when defending free kicks. If the free kick is anywhere near the penalty area, then there is a good chance the attacking team will look to shoot on goal. In these situations the goalkeeper has a vital role. They will need to decide if they want a wall and, if so, how many players they require in it. Usually the outside player in the wall will turn around and line up the wall with the goalkeeper, who advises them where they want the 'first' player to be. Other players then join the wall accordingly.

Defending teams also like to have a player who does not mark any particular attacker, but has a role to charge the ball down as soon as the kick is taken. This player hopes to block the ball before it reaches the wall or goalkeeper. They will need to be quick, brave, determined and prepared for the ball to hit them where it hurts. Are you this kind of player?

Quote	'The success I have at free kicks is five per cent skill and 95 per cent successful imagery.' Gianfranco Zola

Imagery, visualization, mental rehearsal and mental practice are all common terms used to describe the process of using your imagination to see yourself performing, say, a free kick or a tackle. If you are able to use all your senses to create an action in your mind before actually carrying out the activity, research has shown that there is more chance of success. This is also true for imagining a positive outcome to a match. If you think and see yourself performing well, you generally will perform well.

Try using imagery yourself in different situations:

- **before going to sleep at night**
- **pre-match**
- **during training**
- **during a break in matches**
- **just before you are about to take a corner, free kick or penalty.**

Setting the offside trap

The offside trap is something that all defending teams should be aware of. However, you need to be very careful about using it, as it can be a risky option. If one player in your team doesn't carry out their role at exactly the right time it can leave attacking players in the clear.

Vital elements for setting the offside trap are communication and anticipation. All defending players need to time their runs so they move past their attackers just before the ball is kicked. If they do not do this together then a striker will be left onside, possibly with the nearest defender running in the wrong direction. If they do it too early, before the ball is passed, the player on the ball will realize the tactic and keep hold of the ball. They will then be in a strong position to dribble past the last line of defence and be clear through on goal.

The defensive players continuously need to be checking their line and communicating with each other. The sweeper or one of the two central defenders will often be the player that calls for the offside trap to be played, either with a shout or with a hand signal. If teams are wishing to utilize the offside trap as a key tactic of their defence, then they need to practise the routine on the training pitch so that all players know their roles and the signals.

Normally the coach or team manager will decide whether they would like you to play with this method. Be careful not to set the offside trap in isolation without your team-mates being prepared.

Key facts to consider

- When the opposition plays the ball back, step up the pitch a few metres.
- If your team plays the long ball out of defence, sprint out as a unit, which may catch attackers offside if the ball is played straight back up to them.
- When setting any offside trap, be careful not to leave the opponent on the ball unchallenged, as they will have dangerous options left open to them – dribbling through on their own or making a pass to an opponent who is running through from a deep position and would not be offside.
- Practise playing the offside trap in training matches. Does it work for your team?

Support play

Even as a defender there will be expectations upon you to get forward and support the player on the ball. Sometimes this support will be from behind or to the side and at other times you may be in front of the player

in possession. Making forward runs is an exciting and important role for defenders to perform. There is a tendency to think that defenders are defensive players and nothing else. However, if you watch top teams and top players perform you will see how often full-backs get forward to join in the attack. The defender getting forward can be decisive in terms of creating the extra player for a 2 v 1 situation and a numerical advantage.

The overlap

A full-back or midfield player who chooses to run past the player in possession into the forward space, often makes the overlapping run. The player in possession is likely to be facing the opposition's goal with their head up and an awareness of what is happening around them. The overlapping player will normally call for the ball as they are running past the player in possession. The 2 v 1 advantage, created by this run, is difficult to defend against.

Figure 9.11 **An overlapping run by a full-back**

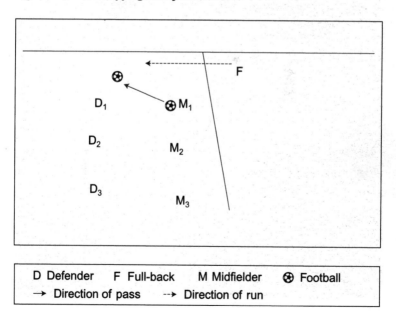

D Defender	F Full-back	M Midfielder	⊕ Football
→ Direction of pass		--→ Direction of run	

DRILL 8: PASS AND OVERLAP

Purpose

To encourage defenders to overlap after making a pass.

You will need:

10 cones

1 football

a minimum of 6 players

Activity

1   Two groups of players face each other at opposite ends of a 10-metre × 20-metre grid.

2   Four cones are positioned across the centre of the grid at equal intervals.

3   P1 passes the ball through the two centre cones to the players at the opposite end of the grid.

4   After making the pass, P1 then sprints around the side cone, representing an overlap run and joins the other group.

Key points for defenders

- Passes should be kept on the ground.
- Use one-touch play whenever possible.
- Make the overlap run purposeful and determined.
- Try to keep the practice continuous.

Progression

A player moves into the centre of the grid to receive the pass and plays a pass into the path of the overlapping player.

Figure 9.12 **Drill 8: Pass and overlap**

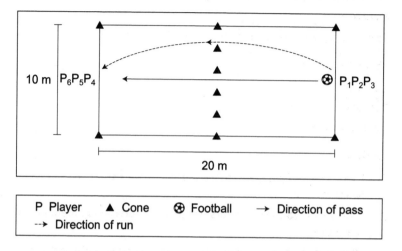

P Player	▲ Cone	⊕ Football	→ Direction of pass
--→ Direction of run			

Third man running

In many ways 'third man running' is similar to the overlap. It is a forward run and is based on a player supporting their team in possession. The only real difference is that it involves three players rather than two. With this particular run, often through the midfield area into the attacking third, a player passes a ball to a holding player, possibly a central striker, who, facing their own goal, lays a ball back to a midfield player. The player who has made the first pass will have set off on an attacking forward run, anticipating the next pass to be a forward one, and the midfield player who receives the lay back passes the ball to this player. The run needs to be purposeful and determined and is an effective tactic for good forward play. It can also see a numerical advantage for the attacking team.

The following practice encourages support play with third man runs.

DRILL 9: THIRD MAN RUNS

Purpose

To encourage players to make third man runs.

You will need:

8 players

4 cones

1 football

Activity

1   Two groups of three players face each other at opposite ends of a 10-metre × 20-metre grid.

2   Two additional players are placed in the centre of the grid to receive passes.

3   P1 passes the ball to P7 and sprints forward following his/her pass.

4   P7 plays a short pass to P8 who then plays the ball into the path of P1.

5   P1 collects it and makes a short pass to P4 before joining the back of the queue.

Key points for defenders

• Quality of pass.

• Quality of lay off, pass in the centre of the grid.

• Purposeful and determined 'third man run'.

• Timing of run and timing of pass.

Figure 9.13 **Drill 9: Third man runs**

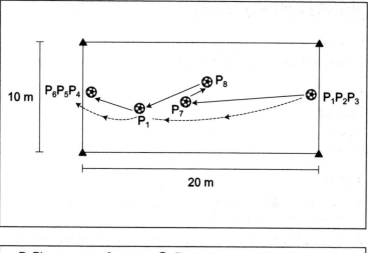

Blind side runs

Another forward run which a full-back should be encouraged to make is a 'blind side run'. It supports the attack and can be a useful tactic in terms of creating goal-scoring opportunities. If a right full-back, for example, was to make this type of run, the ball position is likely to be on the left side of the pitch in a reasonably advanced position, with his/her team in position. Often teams defending with the ball on one side of the pitch can watch the ball, rather than what is going on around them. If this situation is happening, the right full-back for the attacking team can try to exploit the space behind the last defender by making a 'blind side' run.

The secret for this to be effective is for the run to be discreet, as late as possible and out of the vision of the defenders. However, the attacking team in possession needs to be able to see the run that the full-back has

Figure 9.14 **A blind side run by a full-back**

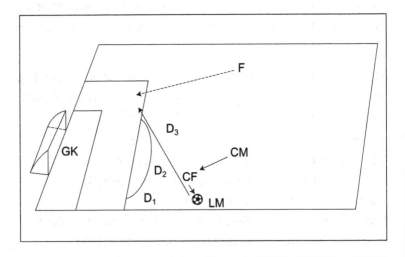

⊕ Football ⇢ Direction of run → Direction of pass D Defender
CF Centre-forward   CM Central midfielder   F Full-back
LM Left midfielder

made, in order to make the pass. A player may use hand signals to make their team aware of their run, without drawing attention to themselves and allowing the defending team to readjust their position.

Passing options for defenders

Whether playing as a full-back or central defender, there will be many times in a game when you will be in possession of the ball. Bearing in mind that the majority of the time you will be in the defending third of the pitch, it is important that you do not lose possession. Good passing skills accompanied by sound decision-making should mean that you can keep possession. Don't forget that you are often the starting point for building an attack.

The diagrams that follow simply illustrate some of the passing options that should be available to you if you are playing at full-back or central defence. These passing options will only occur if your team-mates work hard to lose their markers and show for the ball. Your responsibility is the quality of the pass they receive and the correct decision, if more than one option is available.

The other options that defenders have when in possession, depending on the situation, are to dribble or run with the ball. Remember, though, that taking a good passing option is often a more effective tactic.

Option 1 – Down the line to player **7** (wide midfielder).

Option 2 – Into the feet of a central midfield player **8**.

Option 3 – Longer pass into the space for central strikers **9**.

Option 4 – Into the feet of a central striker **10**.

Option 5 – Into the feet of the central defender for a switch of play **5**.

Option 6 – The diagonal switch of play to wide midfielder **11**.

The defender should expect all players showing to receive a pass to make an initial run to 'shake off' their marker, giving them more time to receive the ball.

Figure 9.15 **Passing options for full-backs**

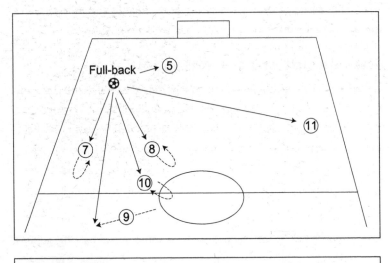

| ⊕ Football | → Direction of pass | --▶ Direction of run |

Figure 9.16 **Passing options for central defenders**

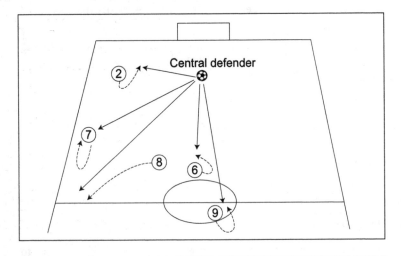

| ⊕ Football | → Direction of pass | --▶ Direction of run |

Option 1 – Into the feet of the wide midfielder **7**.

Option 2 – Into the feet of the full-back **2**.

Option 3 – Into the space over the top of wide midfielder for central midfield runner **8** – diagonal pass.

Option 4 – Into the feet of a central midfielder **6**.

Option 5 – Same pass as option 3, but instead of central midfielder making one run, player **7**, wide midfielder, makes a run towards the central defender then turns quickly to exploit the space behind their maker.

Option 6 – Into the feet of the central striker **9**.

The central defender should expect all players showing to receive a pass to make an initial run to try to 'shake off' any marker, giving them more time to receive the ball.

Top tip

As a defender, relax on the ball and enjoy possession.

In order to practise techniques for passing down the line or across the pitch, the following two drills may be useful for you and your team-mates to try.

DRILL 10: HIT THE DIAGONAL

Purpose

To improve the defender's ability to make accurate diagonal passes.

You will need:

a minimum of 6 players and a goalkeeper

several footballs

half a pitch

a goal

4 cones

Activity

1   Using half the pitch, including a goal and a goalkeeper, two groups of players practise making accurate diagonal passes across the pitch.

2   Two players represent full-backs FB1 and FB2, who take it in turns to play a 1–2 with a server.

3   They then make a long diagonal pass to an advancing wide midfielder (WM1–3 take turns) who tries to take the pass in their run and shoot on goal.

4   Work both sides by alternating sides of the pitch for FBs and WMs.

Key points for defenders

*   Good passing technique.

*   Accuracy of the pass first, then develop the weight of the pass.

*   Into the path of, rather than behind, the wide midfielder.

Figure 9.17 **Drill 10: Hit the diagonal**

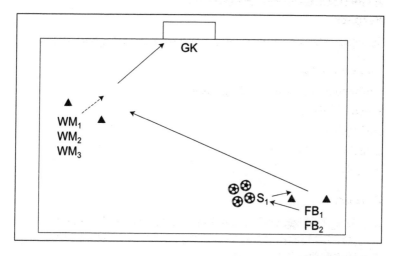

⊕ Football	▲ Cone	⇢ Direction of run	→ Direction of pass
WM Wide Midfielder	FB Full-back	GK Goalkeeper	S Server

Progression

- Apply pressure to the full-backs by adding a player to act as a defender.

- Carry out the practice on both sides of the pitch, practising right and left foot passes.

DRILL 11: DOWN THE CHANNEL

Purpose

To improve the defender's ability to make accurate passes down the channel.

Activity

1   Two full-backs are positioned in a small grid to the side of a penalty area.

2   A server, approximately ten metres from the grid, passes the ball into the grid to one of the full-backs.

3   The server then follows their pass to apply pressure to the two full-backs who have to make four passes between them before making their accurate pass down the channel to the target player.

Key points for defenders

• Creating the time and space to make the pass.

Figure 9.18 **Drill 11: Down the channel**

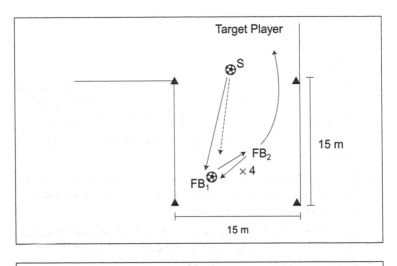

⊗ Football   ▲ Cone   ⤏ Direction of run   → Direction of pass
FB   Full-back   S Server

- Accuracy of the pass.
- Good movement, angle of support and distance between the two full-backs.

Keeping possession

As a defender you will often find yourself in possession and under pressure. On these occasions you rely on your team-mates around you to help you on the ball by providing support (angle and distance). It is important that you and your fellow defenders work on improving your technical ability to keep possession as a unit when put under pressure.

The following drill is designed to assist you play from the back.

DRILL 12: BACK FOUR UNDER PRESSURE

Purpose

To develop the back four's ability to play and pass from the back.

You will need:

half a pitch   1 football

12 players and a goalkeeper   bibs

a goal

Activity

1 This drill takes place in half of the pitch and includes a goal and goalkeeper. It is designed to improve the ability of the back four players to keep possession and then build an attack.

2 Four defenders start just in front of the penalty area, with four attackers on the half-way line.

3 Two attackers start the attack by passing the ball to one of the defenders and follow their pass to put pressure on the back four, creating a 4 v 2 situation.

4 The players' objective is to score, while the defenders need to make four passes before they can make a pass to any of the attackers waiting on the half-way line.

5   A1 – A8 waiting on the halfway line, alternate as attackers to give periods of rest for players taking part.

Key points for defenders

- Defending players in possession must support each other with good angle and distance of support.

- Look to switch play and miss out a player, when making passes across the pitch.

- Play with width so that the two attackers are having to cover a larger area.

- Need a good first touch receiving the ball, redirecting it out of your feet, for the pass to be made.

- Move quickly and offer support after making a pass.

Progression

- Restrict defenders to two touches.

- Increase the number of attackers from two to three.

Figure 9.19 **Drill 12: Back four under pressure**

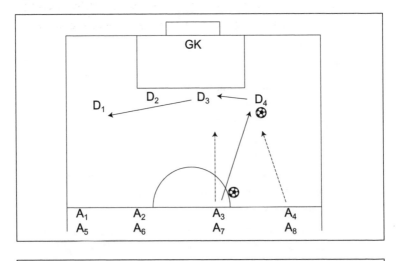

⊕ Football   --▸ Direction of run   → Direction of pass   D Defender
A Attacker   GK Goalkeeper

Switching play in defence

Switching play can take place anywhere on the pitch by any player. As a defender you should understand the reasons why a switch of play can be an advantage to your team. One of the main times that a switch of play occurs is when a team is attacking down one flank and the forward pass is blocked, either by lack of space or too many defenders. A good tactic is to think about passing the ball infield to a central defender or midfield player who can then play across the pitch. By playing a quick long ball to the other wing you are changing the focus of the play. You may catch out your opponents who may not be organized and ready to deal with the situation.

Top tip

If you are going to switch play, make it happen fast, before the opportunity has gone, and try to pass the ball into the space for your team-mate to run onto.

Drill 13 below assists you and your fellow defenders to practise passing the ball across the back four, concentrating on distance of support and balance and switching play.

DRILL 13: STAY BALANCED AND SWITCH PLAY

Purpose

For back four players to practise the distance and support when in possession.

You will need:

5 cones

1 football

a minimum of 4 players

Activity

1   Five cones are placed within a 20-metre × 50-metre area, equally spaced across the width.

2   The practice starts with the right back (RB) passing the ball to the first central defender (CD) and then following their pass.

3   This continues across the pitch until the left back (LB) receives the ball.

4   The left back dribbles it to cone 5 and then turns and starts the practice again going the other way across the pitch.

Key points for defenders

- Once the pass has been made, players should quickly take up a new position near to the next cone.
- Keep the equal spacing between the four defenders.
- Stay as a unit.
- Central defenders should drop off slightly to receive the ball.
- Firm accurate passes.
- Good first touch.
- Let the ball run across your body as you receive it.

Progression

- Players can miss players out and not necessarily pass in the same sequence. For example, miss out one of the central defenders.

Figure 9.20 **Drill 13: Stay balanced and switch play**

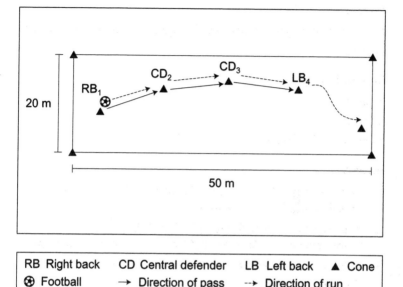

- Introduce a goalkeeper and use them as part of the practice to make a back five.
- Pass with right and left foot.

Counter attacking from defence

There are many different ways that a side will build up an attack. We have already mentioned that, as a defender, you will often be the starting point of the attack. One of the most exciting forms of attack is the counter attack and defenders have their part to play. It is a match-winning tactic, and sides such as Arsenal are experts at it. In simple terms it involves turning defensive play into attack with a fast incisive break. Features of a fast counter attack include:

- One quick short pass followed by a long pass, or simply one long pass.

- Players supporting their team-mates quickly.

- Any space in front of a player is attacked.

- Forward runs are diagonal rather than straight to avoid running offside.

- Players have good technique and are physically fit and fast.

Summary

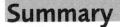

- The basic principles of defending are pressure, support and cover.

- When defending set plays, get organized as quickly as possible and concentrate until the danger has passed.

- As a defender you will be expected to get forward at crucial times to support the player on the ball.

- Defenders need a range of passing skills and to be good at decision-making to keep possession.

Self-tester

- What are the two main defensive methods that a team may choose to use?

- Describe 'high-pressure' defence.

- What is 'third man running'?

Action plan

Discuss these tactics and ideas with your coach and agree on a coaching plan for ten weeks. Try to evaluate your performance so you can identify the areas of your game which you may need to concentrate on.

Part 4

Developing your game

Chapter 10

Parents, coaches and clubs

THIS CHAPTER WILL:

- Help you to understand how important parents or carers are to your development as a player.
- Explain the roles played by the coach and parent.
- Show how you can work successfully with your coach.
- Provide guidance on choosing a club.

Parent power

One of the biggest influences on your football interest and involvement will be your parents or carers. Your coach or a teacher at school may fine-tune your dribbling skills and improve your passing techniques, but your parents will have the major impact on your desire, attitudes, values and ambitions.

Research has shown that the interest and support of parents is vital to a young player's participation in sport. It has, however, also shown that much of the pressure and anxiety that young players feel in sport come from their parents. You need to be aware of this; some of the influence of your parents on your football experience will be positive and constructive, but some will not.

Positive and negative effects

Most parents have the best intentions in mind when they support and help their child to become footballers, whether for the local park team or for a professional club. However, these good intentions can sometimes lose their way as parents get involved with the emotional roller-coaster ride of junior football. We have all witnessed the parents who shout and scream from the touchline, following every movement of their own child, with no awareness of the other players in the team. Goals, results and their child's involvement in the game are all-important, with criticism as likely as encouragement when talking to their child following a game.

These types of parents believe that they are supporting their eight-year-old, but instead they may be building up possible problems for them. They probably mean well – they just want their son or daughter to succeed, but they just get too animated and involved. So why does this happen?

Parents have a strong desire to 'make things right' for their son or daughter, which can be taken too far, however well intentioned. A belief that there is a right and a wrong way to do things can lead to confrontation, for example, by telling a child what he or she should have done, rather than respecting them and encouraging the child to work things out for themselves.

Many parents are reliving their sporting experience through their child, which is one reason why they want as many opportunities open to their child as possible. If their son or daughter fails, it is a reflection of their own sporting ability, or inability, and it is felt acutely. Once again, the intentions of trying to maximize opportunities are good but the effect when seen to be a failure can be negative. The pressure on a player of losing or playing badly can be doubled if their parent reacts in a frustrated and angry way.

Quote | 'The importance of not pressuring athletes to "win early" in their careers, but to teach values such as hard work, optimism and a "can do" attitude seem paramount . . . At the same time, parents emphasized the attitude "if you are going to do it, do it right". They also modelled a hard work ethic, held high (but reasonable) expectations and standards for their child and emphasized a "stick to it" attitude.'

Dan Gould, 'The Development of psychological talent in US Olympic champions', 2002

It is not easy to be a good parent of a competitive football player. As a player you need to be aware of this, and encourage parents to:

- **be supportive without telling you how to do or not do something (unless you ask for help)**
- **listen . . . properly, without doing ten other things at the same time (parents are very busy people!)**
- **focus on the way you play and whether you're having fun and improving as a footballer**
- **motivate you to work hard and put in effort.**

Role models

So, do parents still have an effect on you as a player as you get older? Certainly, the role a parent plays in the early years will help to shape your interest and attitude. This is not just through supporting you, but also through watching football in a wider sense. Sitting together to watch a match on television or going to a match together helps forge a bond and gives an opportunity to share thoughts on the way the game is played. For example:

- **How do you think Joseph Yobo played today?**
- **Would you play Jones in that position?**
- **Have you seen how much space their midfield has been allowed?**
- **Do you think that was a fair tackle?**

Informal chatting around questions like these helps you to gain a keen understanding of the way the game is played, the positions, the attitudes, the pace and the roles of the individual players within each team. This can all be related back to your own experience as a player, and will have an influence on the way you play.

All through your development as a player you have hopefully had the backing and support of your parents. It may be in a small way, such as making your drink or washing your kit, or in a much greater way such as managing your team. As you mature and develop as a player this role can be reversed, with you as a player giving your parents the opportunity to feel involved. After training, talk to them about the session. What did you learn? How did you feel? Was it an enjoyable session? Don't wait for questions; show them that you value their interest. After a match, talk about the way the game went, the highs and lows and, if they watched, ask them what they thought about the match. Try to be positive and you are likely to get a positive response.

Most importantly, you are the link between your coach and your parents. Any information given to you by your coach concerning dates of matches, kick-off times or changes to training needs to be passed on to your parents. It can be incredibly frustrating as a coach or manager if information isn't passed on and only six players turn up at a rearranged match. This works both ways – any messages from your parents, perhaps concerning holidays away, need to be passed on to your coach or manager.

Coaching principles

Football coaches come in many shapes, sizes and styles, but they all share one quality: a desire to improve their players and their team. Some have more success than others in achieving this! All coaches have beliefs and opinions about what coaching is and how coaches can help players. Many will have been playing football for more years than they care to mention, others will be huge football fans, with a fantastic knowledge about football. Some will be trained and qualified FA coaches, others will be willing volunteers with no qualifications but plenty of enthusiasm.

For all these types of coaches, much of their success or failure depends on their principles – their ethics, sense of fair play and their codes of behaviour. These have a direct impact on the players. You may have been a player in a number of teams, with a variety of different coaches and each will have developed their own style of coaching. Think about your coach, or a coach from a previous team, and consider these questions about their coaching principles:

- Does the coach shout from the touchline? Is it constructive?
- Are you encouraged to enjoy the game?
- Is winning all-important?
- Are players punished for a poor performance?
- What is the view of your coach on swearing?
- Does the coach communicate well with all the players?
- What is the view of your coach on cheating?
- Are you encouraged to accept refereeing decisions?
- Do all players have a chance to play?

The principles of your coach will affect the way you play the game. The principles a coach upholds will be evident in their behaviour towards others, and in how they expect you as a player to behave towards them.

As well as playing as a footballer, you may want to coach a team in the future, so bear the following principles in mind.

Principles of successful coaching might include:

- respecting the needs of individuals and treating all players fairly
- developing independence by encouraging players and other coaches to accept responsibility for their own behaviour
- the development of individuals as people as well as football players
- the development of mutual trust, respect and commitment
- positive acknowledgement of progress and achievement
- communication with players, coaches, parents and other helpers
- promoting fair play within the laws of the game and respecting the dignity of opponents and officials
- accepting responsibility for the conduct of players and encouraging positive social and moral behaviours
- maintaining confidentiality of information when appropriate to do so
- displaying high personal standards of behaviour, dress and communication
- ensuring as far as possible the safety and health of players
- developing personal competence as a coach.

(Based on the FA Sport and Recreation 'Values Statement for Coaching, Teaching and Instructing', 2000)

Working with a coach

If you ask a coach what they value most in a player, many will state the ability to listen. Players are more likely to improve their skills and techniques by concentrating when they are asked to listen to any instructions. Any information or advice given is then internalized and can be transferred to the physical action. Obviously this can be a problem if the coach isn't particularly inspiring or if other players around have a poor attitude. However, this is an important life skill as it concerns a feeling of respect for others, and will say a lot about you as a person as well as a player. If you listen well, you are also likely to ask more questions, sharing the responsibility for improving yourself as a player and the team as a whole.

Talking to the coach, listening, asking questions . . . this is all about communication. It is a two-way process, and many players forget to respond positively to their coach. So be friendly and supportive, talk to the coach if things are going wrong or going well, and don't forget to thank your coach at the end of a training session or match.

Effort is another quality highly rated by coaches. If you work hard in training, try things out, and concentrate on improving your skills and technique, you will get more out of the training and are likely to increase your enjoyment. Show the same effort and commitment in matches and you will definitely be a valued team member, for the other players and the coach. This is particularly true if things aren't going well in a match. If winning and losing is all-important, with too much emphasis being placed on the result, it is very easy to 'give up' when being beaten. There is a sense of failure and some individuals are likely to withdraw their effort and behave in a negative way to 'protect' their own perceived ability at football.

These 'ego-oriented' individuals see success in terms of winning and out-performing others, with even greater success if they put in little effort to win. A 'task-oriented' player sees success in terms of getting better by trying harder. Research has shown that these players will remain motivated even when they are losing, because success is not based purely on the result, but on trying hard to improve. For example, a centre-forward who misses a few chances will continue to run into space in the attacking third of the field and accept the responsibility of taking shots at goal. If this is an 'ego-oriented' player, they are likely to put in less effort and drift further and further back after missing a few chances. Coaches find this behaviour difficult to understand, but it is often based on a player's early experiences of playing in a team. It is not too late to change, but you need to be aware of the differences. It is also worth pointing out that top professional footballers have a mixture of high-ego and high-task orientation – they have a strong desire to win and put in a huge amount of effort to improve as a player. What sort of player are you – 'ego-oriented' or 'task-oriented'?

Choosing a club

Finding a football club that is right for you can be a difficult decision and you are likely to need the support of your parents. The easiest option is to follow your friends to a particular club or to join your nearest one. Although this can often be the best reason for choosing a club, other factors should be considered. To begin with, think of the sort of football you want to play and ask yourself the following questions:

- How much commitment do you want to give to training and matches?
- Are you able to play regularly on a Saturday or Sunday?
- How far are you willing to travel?
- What standard do you want to achieve?
- Do you want to play for a team that has a fun 'everyone plays' philosophy, or do you want a competitive environment (or a bit of both)?

Once you've considered this, make a list of the clubs that are available to you:

- **Contact your local County Football Association or local organization. They will be able to provide you with a list of clubs and programmes being offered in your area.**
- **Ask friends and their parents and get their views.**
- **Ask at your school, as many clubs have developed excellent relationships with their local school.**
- **Look in the local press and on the Internet for contact details of clubs in your localilty.**

Once you are ready to contact or visit a club, find out the background information on the club by checking its website, looking at any brochures or by talking to club officials. Consider the following:

- **Is the club FA affiliated and part of a local league organization?**
- **Has the club got 'Charter Standard' or 'Community Club' status?**
- **How experienced and qualified are the coaches?**
- **Do they cater for a range of age groups for boys and girls?**
- **What are the facilities at the club like?**
- **Does the club have social and fund-raising events?**
- **What is the club's philosophy?**
- **What are the selection procedures? (For example, does missing training mean that a player is left out of the team?)**
- **Does the club have a code of conduct? (See pages 222–30).**
- **Does the club follow the FA child protection procedures? (This should be a definite yes!)**
- **Who are the club officials – chair, secretary, treasurer etc?**

In England the FA has a club recognition programme – Charter Standard Clubs. If a club you are looking at has this status, then that will certainly help answer a lot of the questions above. To receive the FA Charter

Standard kitemark, clubs must demonstrate safe, quality practice. This includes:

- **qualified coaches**
- **child protection trained staff and policy**
- **codes of conduct**
- **fair play.**

The next step is to visit the club. Here are a few tips on what to look out for on your first visit, perhaps to watch training or a match:

- **Is there a welcoming atmosphere?**
- **Do the players look like they are enjoying the football?**
- **Are there parents watching or do they keep away?**
- **What is the relationship like between the coach and players?**
- **Is there a good coach to player ratio? Generally, this should be two coaches per squad, with a maximum 1:16 ratio.**

Once you are a member of a team, try to get involved with the club in a broader way. Go along to any social events and support them in fund-raising activities. If they need volunteer help in, say, running a mini-soccer event, put your name forward. The more you get involved, the more you will get out of being part of the club.

Becoming a coach

Some of you may have a desire to continue your interest in football beyond just playing the game. Coaching football is a tremendous way to give back to grassroots players some of the skills and attributes that you have developed over the years. Once you make a start on the coaching journey you will become a valued member of the community and, for some of you, it may even influence the path your career takes.

As soon as you reach the age of 16, you are able to start your coaching development by taking the FA's level 1 coaching award. Although you may feel you have a good understanding of the game, the course looks at much more than just training drills and tactics and is a valuable exercise for anyone looking to play a role in coaching. It is also the first rung on the ladder and an important one for providing you with the FA philosophy for coaches.

For those interested in coaching, Table 10.1 shows the development of courses and awards for coaches in England.

Codes of conduct

The Football Association expects certain standards from all those involved in the game, whether players, officials, parents or coaches, at whatever level of play. A set of guidelines for clubs has been issued, which outlines the standards expected from the FA.

FA Code of Conduct for football

1 General

Football is the national game. All those involved with the game at every level and whether as a player, match official, coach or administrator, have a responsibility, above and beyond compliance with the law, to act according to the highest standards of integrity, and to ensure that the reputation of the game is, and remains high. This code applies to all those involved in football under the auspices of the Football Association.

2 Community

Football at all levels is a vital part of a community. Football will take into account community feelings when making decisions.

3 Equality

Football is opposed to discrimination of any form and will promote measures to prevent it, in whatever form, from being expressed.

Table 10.1 **Courses and awards for coaches in England**

Course	For whom	Prerequisites	Where
Coaching Level 1	Coaches of young players.	Open entry course for anybody over 16 years of age. You don't need any experience, just an interest in the game and motivation to improve your knowledge.	Locally run courses managed by County FA's as well as residentially run courses at approved FA centres.
Coaching Level 2	Coaches with some experience at any level with regular participation.	Open entry course for anybody over 16 years of age with regular practical experience of participation in football.	Locally run courses managed by County FA's as well as residentially run courses at approved FA centres.
Coaching Level 3 /UEFA 'B'	Coaches that are working with a team over an extensive period.	Anybody over 18 years of age. Candidates must hold the Level 2 Coaching Certificate.	Locally run courses managed by County FA's as well as residentially run courses at approved FA centres.
UEFA 'A'	Coaches with experience at representative level.	Candidates must hold the Level 3 /UEFA 'B' Certificate in Coaching.	Nationally run course that takes place residentially at approved FA centres.

For more information and to enrol on a course visit www.TheFA.com/FALearning

4 Participants

Football recognizes the sense of ownership felt by those who participate at all levels of the game. This includes those who play, those who coach or help in any way, and those who officiate, as well as administrators and supporters. Football is committed to appropriate consultation.

5 Young people

Football acknowledges the extent of its influence over young people and pledges to set a positive example.

6 Propriety

Football acknowledges that public confidence demands the highest standards of financial and administrative behaviour within the game, and will not tolerate corruption or improper practices.

7 Trust and respect

Football will uphold a relationship of trust and respect between all involved in the game, whether they are individuals, clubs or other organizations.

8 Violence

Football rejects the use of violence of any nature by anyone involved in the game.

9 Fairness

Football is committed to fairness in its dealings with all involved in the game.

10 Integrity and fair play

Football is committed to the principle of playing to win consistent with fair play.

FA Code of Conduct for coaches

1 Coaches are the key to the establishment of ethics in football. The concept of ethics and their attitude directly affects the behaviour of players under their supervision. Coaches are,

therefore, expected to pay particular attention to the moral aspects of their conduct. Coaches have to be aware that almost all of their everyday decisions and choice, as well as strategic targets, have ethical implications.

2   It is natural that winning constitutes a basic concern for coaches. This code is not intended to conflict with that. However, the code calls for coaches to disassociate themselves from a 'win at all costs' attitude.

3   Increased responsibility is requested from coaches involved in coaching young people. The health, safety, welfare and moral education of young people are a first priority, before the achievement or the reputation of the club, coach or parent.

4   Set out below is the FA Coaches Association Code of Conduct (which reflects the standards expressed by the National Coaching Foundation and the National Association of Sports Coaches) which forms the benchmark for all involved in coaching:

   a   Coaches must respect the rights, dignity and worth of each and every person and treat each equally within the context of the sport.

   b   Coaches must place the well-being and safety of each player above all other considerations, including the development of performance.

   c   Coaches must adhere to all guidelines laid down by governing bodies.

   d   Coaches must develop an appropriate working relationship with each player based on mutual trust and respect.

   e   Coaches must not exert undue influence to obtain personal benefit or reward.

   f   Coaches must encourage and guide players to accept responsibility for their own behaviour and performance.

   g   Coaches must ensure that the activities they direct or advocate are appropriate for the age, maturity, experience and ability of players.

   h   Coaches should, at the outset, clarify with the players (and, where appropriate, parents) exactly what is expected of them and also what they are entitled to expect from their coach.

i   Coaches must cooperate fully with other specialists (e.g. other coaches, officials, sports scientists, doctors, and physiotherapists) in the best interests of the players.

j   Coaches must always promote the positive aspects of the sport (e.g. fair play) and never condone violations of the laws of the game, behaviour contrary to the spirit of the laws of the game or relevant rules and regulations or the use of prohibited substances or techniques.

k   Coaches must consistently display high standards of behaviour and appearance.

l   Coaches must not use or tolerate inappropriate language.

FA Code of Conduct for players

1   Players are the most important people in the sport. Playing for the team, and for the team to win, is the most fundamental part of the game. But not winning at any cost – fair play and respect for others is of utmost importance.

2   This code is derived from one that focuses on players involved in top-class football. Nevertheless, the key concepts in the code are valid for players at all levels.

a   **Obligations towards the game**

A player should:

- Make every effort to develop their own sporting abilities, in terms of skill, technique, tactics and stamina.

- Give maximum effort and strive for the best possible performance during a game, even if his team is in a position where the desired result has already been achieved.

- Set a positive example to others, particularly young players and supporters.

- Avoid all forms of gamesmanship and time wasting.

- Always have regard for the best interests of the game, including where publicly expressing an opinion on the game and any particular aspect of it, including others involved in the game.

- Not use inappropriate language.

b Obligations towards one's own team

A player should:

- Make every effort consistent with fair play and the laws of the game to help his own team win.

- Resist any influence which might, or might be seen to, bring into question his commitment to the team winning.

c Respect for the laws of the game and competition rules

A player should:

- Know and abide by the laws, rules and spirit of the game, and the competition rules.

- Accept success and failure, victory and defeat, equally.

- Resist any temptation to take banned substances or use banned techniques.

d Respect towards opponents

A player should:

- Treat opponents with due respect at all times, irrespective of the result of the game.

- Safeguard the physical fitness of opponents, avoid violence and rough play, and help injured opponents.

e Respect towards match officials

A player should:

- Accept the decisions of the match officials without protest.

- Avoid words or actions that may mislead match officials.

- Show due respect towards match officials.

f **Respect towards team officials**

A player should:

- Abide by the instructions of their coach and team officials, provided they do not contradict the spirit of the code.

- Show due respect towards the team officials of the opposition.

g **Obligations towards the supporters**

A player should:

- Show due respect to the interests of supporters.

FA Code of Conduct for team officials

This code applies to all team/club officials (although some elements may not apply to all officials).

1 Obligations towards the game

The team official should:

- Set a positive example for others, particularly young players and supporters.

- Promote and develop his own team, having regard to the interests of the players, supporters and the reputation of the national game.

- Share knowledge and experience when invited to do so, taking into account the interest of the body that has requested this rather than personal interests.

- Avoid all forms of gamesmanship.

- Show due respect to match officials and others involved in the game.

- Always have regard for the best interests of the game, including where publicly expressing an opinion of the game and any particular aspect of it, including others involved in the game.

- Not use or tolerate inappropriate language.

2 Obligations towards the team

The team official should:

- Make every effort to develop the sporting, technical and tactical levels of the club/team, and to obtain the best results for the team, using all permitted means.
- Give priority to the interests of the team over individual interests.
- Resist all illegal or unsporting influences, including banned substances and techniques.
- Promote ethical principles.
- Show due respect for the interests of the players, coaches and officials, their own club/team and others.

3 Obligations towards supporters

The team official should:

- Show due respect for the interests of supporters.

4 Respect towards match officials

The team official should:

- Accept the decisions of the match officials without protest.
- Avoid words or actions that may mislead a match official.
- Show due respect towards match officials.

FA Code of Conduct for parents/spectators

1 Parents/spectators have a great influence on children's enjoyment and success in football. All children play football because they first and foremost love the game – it's fun. Remember that however good a child becomes at football within the club it is important to reinforce the message to parents/spectators that positive encouragement will contribute to:

- children enjoying football
- a sense of personal achievement
- self-esteem
- improving the child's skills and techniques.

2　A parent's/spectator's expectations and attitudes have a significant bearing on a child's attitude towards:

- other players
- officials
- managers
- spectators.

3　Parents/spectators will be positive and encouraging towards all children, not just their own.

4　Parents/spectators are encouraged to:

- Applaud the opposition as well as our own teams.
- Avoid coaching during the game.
- Refrain from shouting and screaming.
- Respect the referee's decisions.
- Give attention to each of the children involved in football, not just the most talented.
- Give encouragement to everyone to participate in football.

5　Parents and spectators should be made aware of these issues together with the club's other adopted codes of conduct and child protection policy.

Summary

- **Your parents or carers will have a major impact on your desire, attitudes, values and ambitions.**

- **Most parents start off with good intentions but may need your support to remain positive.**

- **Much of the success or failure of a coach depends on their principles – their ethics, sense of fair play and codes of behaviour.**

- **Effort and good communication from players are highly valued by coaches.**

- **If you are in a position where you need to choose a club, put some time and research into choosing one that is right for you.**

Self-tester

- Give three ways to involve your parents positively in your interest in football.
- Describe some of the principles of successful coaching. Give four examples.
- What are the requirements for a club to achieve Charter Standard?

Action plan

Consider your attitudes and behaviour during training sessions and matches. For the next four matches and training sessions make a conscious effort to listen carefully, communicate more and put in more effort. Monitor the difference this makes to you as a player.

References:

Motivation: More than a Question of Winning and Losing (1999)
Darren C. Treasure, Assistant Professor of Sport and Exercise Psychology, Arizona State University.

You may find the following books helpful:
The Official FA Guide: A Parent's Guide to Football by Les Howie
The Official FA Guide to Basic Team Coaching by Les Reed
The Official FA Guide to Basic Refereeing by John Baker
The Official FA Guide to Running a Club by Les Howie

Chapter 11

Evaluating your performance

THIS CHAPTER WILL:
- Explain how a goal-setting programme can improve your game.
- Show the three stages for implementing a goal-setting programme.
- Give a practical example of a weekly goal-setting diary.

Why set goals?

Sport psychologists have identified goal-setting as an effective way to help players prepare for competition and improve technical, physical and mental performance. It involves the establishment of specific targets that show what a player, with or without the involvement of a coach, is striving to achieve.

Goal-setting should be seen as a method of helping you to develop your areas of weakness and maintain your strengths. This chapter focuses specifically on the development of the individual rather than the team.

Types of goal

Training goals

Training goals can improve performance by directing attention towards specific aspects of personal development as well as by generating the effort needed to make progress. Training goals are often organized through a framework that features long- and short-term goals (see below).

Competition goals

'Process' goals can be used to influence the way you approach games. They can focus on specific tasks before a match, such as closing down quickly or being aware of movement off the ball. It is important to focus your attention on the process rather than the outcome of the match.

Long-term goals

These identify what a player or coach wants to achieve. They are usually stated in general terms and reflect a player's aspirations and ambitions. An example could be for a player to establish themselves as a 'regular' in his/her local team, or to successfully recover from an injury.

Short-term goals

These are more precise and associated with daily/weekly 'action steps'. Short-term goals and 'action steps' can influence what takes place at your team's training session or they may relate to your individual practice time.

Short-term goals relate to practical action which can lead to achieving your long-term goals. An example might be to improve short passing skills.

Statistics

Goal-setting and targets are used by professional football clubs to help the development of the players at their academies and centres of excellence.

It may be better understood if players think of the short-term and long-term goals being linked as a staircase (see figure 11.1). At the top of the staircase is the long-term goal, with the short-term goals being represented by the progression of stairs. Achieving short-term goals improves the likelihood that long-term goals will be reached.

Figure 11.1 **An example of a goal-setting staircase**

Establish myself as a 'regular' player in my local team.

Maintain concentration for the full game.

Improve fitness level.

Improve accuracy of passing.

Improve communication on the pitch.

Improve ball control.

In simple terms:

commitment to action steps = short-term goals achieved = long-term goals realized

Top tip

Be realistic! You need to be realistic about the amount of time and effort you can put into a goal-setting programme.

The three stages for implementing a goal-setting programme

Before setting a programme, it is important that you have spent some time evaluating your game – your strengths, weaknesses and long-term goals. You can do this on your own or, even better, by involving a supportive parent or coach. The coach or parent can oversee the programme and alter and develop it over time. Table 11.1 sets out the three stages involved in a goal-setting programme.

Table 11.1 **Goal-setting stages**

Stage 1	Stage 2	Stage 3
Establish the way forward	**Set goals**	**Monitor, maintain and evaluate**
Meeting/discussion.	Goal-setting programme should come from the meeting/discussion.	Formal or informal meetings to reflect on progress and consider any changes.
Consider your strengths and weaknesses.		
The coach, if involved, should become familiar with your views about your own ability as well as any personal targets.	Establish long-terms goals.	Whenever possible, record progress in writing.
	Identify short-term goals (what has to be done to achieve the long-term goals).	Check the time you have given and how long it is taking to achieve short- and long-term goals.
Coach should share his/her views on how you could improve.	Make sure the goals are:	
	Specific	This stage allows for new challenges and targets to be set.
	Measurable	
	Achievable/adjustable	
	Realistic/recorded	
	Time phased.	

> ## Top tip
>
> Make sure that when you set a goal programme, the goals are SMART.

Keeping a goal-setting diary

It is a good idea to keep a weekly goal-setting diary. This is an example of one that has been completed. Use this model to start your own diary:

WEEKLY GOAL-SETTING DIARY   **DATE:**
Short-term goal for this week:
Develop my short passing skills

Action steps	Thoughts
Monday	
Work with team-mate/coach on controlling and passing. Use both feet, two touch only.	*Passing with my right foot is good, though I am still weak with my left.*
Tuesday	
No training.	
Wednesday	
Five-a-side match with team-mates. *Goal – I will try to play two touch when in possession.*	*My accuracy of passes had improved. I enjoyed the match and was pleased with my performance.*
Thursday	
Team training session. Coach to organize short passing drills. *Goal: in drills I will play one touch.*	*My passing was accurate and sharp, particularly with my right foot. I am starting to feel more confident.*
Friday	
School match. *Goal – accurate passing and quick decisions on the ball.*	*Satisfied with my performance as short passing had improved though coach felt I could make quicker decisions.*

Summary

- **Goal-setting can help you to organize your training and ensure that important areas of development have a focus.**

- **It is important to establish long- and short-term goals for training and to use process type goals as part of your preparation for playing competitive football.**

- **Goal-setting should be written down and reviewed on a regular basis.**

- **The more effort you put into your goal-setting programme the greater the chance of success in improving your play.**

Self-tester

- What are the three key stages in a goal-setting programme?
- Describe action steps.
- What does SMART stand for?

Action plan

Consider developing your own goal-setting programme using the three-stage approach covered in this chapter. Start by planning a diary and arranging a meeting with your coach.

You may find *The Official FA Guide to Psychology for Football* by Dr Andy Cale useful.

Index

Master the Game
Goalkeeper

Achieve your potential

Master the Game: Goalkeeper gives you the skills and essential advice
you need to perfect this key position. It helps you master the specific
skills and techniques that are fundamental to becoming a great
goalkeeper, and covers nutritional, fitness and psychological aspects of
player performance.

This book enables you to:
- **understand the key principles of play**
- **prepare for the game**
- **improve your skills, from throwing to diving saves**
- **learn from your match performance.**

Packed full of indispensable tips and techniques, this book will soon
enhance your ability and increase your enjoyment of the world's
greatest game.

Paul Broadbent is the manager and coach of an under-16s
football team and a widely published author. **Andrew Allen** is a
development manager for school sport and an FA qualified coach.

Master the Game
Midfielder

Achieve your potential

Master the Game: Midfielder gives you the skills and essential advice
you need to perfect this key position. It helps you master the specific
skills and techniques that are fundamental to becoming a great
midfielder, and covers nutritional, fitness and psychological aspects of
player performance.

This book enables you to:
- **understand the key principles of play**
- **prepare for the game**
- **improve your skills, from ball control to passing**
- **learn from your match performance.**

Packed full of indispensable tips and techniques, this book will soon
enhance your ability and increase your enjoyment of the world's
greatest game.

Paul Broadbent is the manager and coach of an under-16s
football team and a widely published author. **Andrew Allen** is a
development manager for school sport and an FA qualified coach.

Master the Game
Striker

Achieve your potential

Master the Game: Striker gives you the skills and essential advice you need to perfect this key position. It helps you master the specific skills and techniques that are fundamental to becoming a great striker, and covers nutritional, fitness and psychological aspects of player performance.

This book enables you to:
- **understand the key principles of play**
- **prepare for the game**
- **improve your skills, from sharp shooting to agility**
- **learn from your match performance.**

Packed full of indispensable tips and techniques, this book will soon enhance your ability and increase your enjoyment of the world's greatest game.

Paul Broadbent is the manager and coach of an under-16s football team and a widely published author. **Andrew Allen** is a development manager for school sport and an FA qualified coach.